The Glory of Love

The Glory of Love

Angela Elwell Hunt

Tyndale House Publishers, Inc.
Wheaton, Illinois

The Cassie Perkins Series

1 No More Broken Promises

2 A Forever Friend

3 A Basket of Roses

4 A Dream to Cherish

5 The Much-Adored Sandy Shore

6 Love Burning Bright

7 Star Light, Star Bright

8 The Chance of a Lifetime

9 The Glory of Love

All Scripture quotations are taken from the *Holy Bible, New International Version*® Copyright © 1973, 1978, 1984 by International Bible Society. Used by permission of Zondervan Publishing House. All rights reserved.

Library of Congress Cataloging-in-Publication Data

Hunt, Angela Elwell, date
    The glory of love / Angela Elwell Hunt.
        p. cm. — (Cassie Perkins ; #9)
    Summary: Cassie finds herself falling in love with her stepbrother's musclebound friend.
    ISBN 0-8423-1119-X
    [1. Stepfamilies—Fiction. 2. Christian life—Fiction.] I. Title.
II. Series: Hunt, Angela Elwell, 1957-   Cassie Perkins ; #9.
PZ7.H9115G1   1993
[Fic]—dc20   92-26554

Printed in the United States of America

99 98 97 96 95 94 93 92
8   7   6   5   4   3   2   1

Important People in My Life, by Cassie Perkins

1. **Glen Perkins,** my dad. ♥♥♥♥♥
   He's a systems analyst for NASA in Houston, Texas. Even though I don't see him much, I think he's the most wonderful man to ever walk the earth.

2. **Claire Louise Perkins Harris,** my mom. ♥♥♥♥♥
   She used to be an interior decorator, but now her new husband, Tom, and baby Steffie take most of her time.

3. **Stephanie Arien Harris,** my new baby sister. Or half sister. Whatever. ♥♥♥♥♥
   The latest addition to our family, baby Steffie actually looks a little like me, even with all that Harris blood in her.

4. **Max Brian Perkins,** my brother. ♥♥♥♥♥!
   Max is a bona fide genius and will be the only twelve-year-old in the eleventh grade at Astronaut High, my school.

5. **Dribbles,** my Chinese pug. ♥♥♥♥
   Wonder Dog. She's eaten two pairs of my shoes, my favorite purse, three of my best cassettes, the extra-special purple pen Chip gave me, *and* my

autographed picture of Chad Reed, the star of "Hollywood High."

6. **Chip McKinnon**, my best friend who also happens to be a boy. ♥ ♥ ♥
   Chip's the best Christian guy I know.

7. **Tom Harris**, my stepfather. ♥ ♥ ♥
   I hated him at first, but even though we don't always agree, he's kind of grown on me.

8. **Nick Harris**, my stepbrother. ♥ ♥
   Nick has been spending time at the neighborhood basketball court instead of hanging around his snooty friends from Princeton Academy. He'll be a senior at Princeton this fall.

9. **Jacob A. Benton** or Uncle Jacob. ♥ ♥ ♥ ♥
   He's the best part about Mom marrying again. Uncle Jake manages the house and talks to me a lot. He's great.

10. **Andrea Milford**, my best friend. ♥ ♥ ♥ ♥
    She was *almost* the next Christie Brinkley, but I guess she's going to hang around Canova Cove and grow up some more before heading out to New York. I'm glad she's staying.

I went through social decompression at Dad's apartment in Houston. I'd just gotten back from two
solid months of being on the road. (I had been tour-
ing and singing with America Now, a group made
up of the eight best singers in the country.) After all
that driving (we must have performed in a hundred
cities . . . well, at least forty) and going from one
city to another, it felt strange to stay in one place.

It felt stranger still to sit in the little guest bedroom of Dad's apartment with my clothes still in my
suitcase. The drawers in the dresser were filled with
my brother Max's stuff. He had been with our father
for most of the summer. I only had a little over a
week to spend with Dad before school started again.
It wasn't enough time to rebuild a relationship. That
was OK, though, because I really didn't have the
energy to work on it.

Don't get me wrong—I love my dad. He's great, even though he lives in Houston now, which means my brother Max and I hardly ever see him. Dad and I have this link that I'll never share with my stepfather, Tom. Maybe it's that Dad and I are both dark-skinned and musical. Even so, whatever link we have isn't strong enough to bind us close together in two weeks after we've been apart for over a year. In fact, though I hated to admit it, as I sat in Dad's guest room, all I really wanted to do was go home to Florida, see my dog, and sleep on my own bed.

Max and Dad were out in the living room playing an electronic game and making weird space sounds. "Hey, guys, what do you say to some pizza tonight?" I called over the pings and rumbles of their computer game. "I'll even order it from Domino's so you won't have to go out, Dad."

"That sounds great, Gypsy Girl," Dad said, turning to wink at me through the doorway. "Get one with mushrooms, onions, and green peppers, will you? I'm watching my figure."

Max burst into giggles, and Dad jiggled his joystick. A loud electronic *ka-boom!* filled the room.

"You're dead, spaceman," Dad told Max. "The old man scores another one. Give it up, Max, you'll never beat your dad at this game."

"Gimme another chance," Max said, resetting the

game. I sighed and lay down on the twin bed, right in the middle of Max's dirty laundry. I shook my head and sighed. *I have a dad who acts like a kid,* I thought, rolling my eyes, *and a little brother who acts like an adult. Together, they're a perfect match.*

After we'd finished off two of Dad's vegetarian pizzas, I called home to talk to Mom. When she answered, I realized how glad I was to hear her voice.

"Hey, Mom, what's new? Have you heard anything from Andrea or Chip? How's Steffie? What's Nick been up to?"

Mom sighed. "Everything's pretty much the same around here," she said. "Steffie's running everywhere now and always getting into trouble. Ever since that kid learned to walk I just can't stop her. How are you, honey? Ready for school?"

"I guess so." I know my voice sounded flat, but I just didn't feel perky. I wouldn't have been able to fool my mother, anyway.

"Lonesome for your friends?"

"Maybe." I did miss Andrea and Chip, my two best friends, but I missed the kids from the America Now singing team, too. We had only sung together for two months, but we'd been around each other day and night for those two months. Without them, I felt like part of my family had been kidnapped. I just wasn't sure where I belonged anymore . . . it was a strange feeling.

One thing was for sure, though: I didn't belong in a Houston apartment.

"I'm ready to come home," I blurted out. "Dad's great, but I'm just tired, Mom. I want to see you all again."

"There's someone here who wants to talk to you," Mom said, a smile in her voice. I heard noises as someone took the receiver.

"Hey, Cassie Girl!" Uncle Jake bellowed, his gruff voice nearly bursting my eardrum. "What's happenin'? When are you coming home?"

"Soon, I hope," I said, a smile creeping onto my face. "That is, if you promise to make your special lasagna for me."

"We'll have it the night you get in, I promise," Uncle Jacob answered. "I got my new Williams-Sonoma catalog today, and there's a recipe for cranberry muffins from authentic American spoon-dried cranberries. I'll make up a batch for you."

"Sounds divine," I giggled. Uncle Jacob was big on gourmet cooking, and the Williams-Sonoma catalog was his favorite reading material. "So what else is new, Uncle Jake?"

Uncle Jacob lowered his voice. "Well, Nicky would

kill me if he heard me tell you this, but he nearly got himself beat up the other day."

"You're kidding!"

"No," Uncle Jake continued in a conspiratorial whisper. "He was down at the park playing a game of pick-up basketball, and this bully, Carmen some-body-or-other, started hassling him. Anyway, Nick thought he was dog meat, but this huge kid stepped in between them and took Nick's side. Ever since then, Nick and this kid have been inseparable."

"Really?" I couldn't picture it. My stepbrother Nick usually hung with preppy jocks—most of his friends were from Princeton Academy, the snooty prep school where he'd be a senior in a couple of weeks. I couldn't imagine him hanging around with one of the neighborhood kids, especially some mus-cle-bound goon.

"Really," Uncle Jake said with a chuckle. "It's not so bad, though. The kid is nice enough. And huge—probably stands six four and is at least two hundred pounds of pure muscle." Now I could hear pure admi-ration in Uncle Jake's voice. "First thing Nick did was invite the kid over for lunch. They're upstairs now, working out on Nick's new set of weights."

"Nick bought *weights?*"

"Yep. This guy is a real iron man, and he's teaching Nick how to pump up." Uncle Jacob chuckled. "It's a hoot, Cassie."

"I can't wait to see the new and improved Nick," I said, laughing. "Does this incredible hunk have a name?"

"Dustin Gray," Uncle Jacob answered. "I expect you'll meet him soon enough. He's over here so much that Tom's threatening to claim him as a tax deduction."

I thought a lot about Dustin Gray as Max and I flew home. I wasn't sure I liked the idea of someone else in our house. I mean, our house was full enough as it was. And while Nick and I had never really been bosom buddies or anything, we were pretty close for a stepbrother and stepsister. But now this Dustin Gray goon was around the house all the time . . . and everybody liked him. Even Uncle Jake, who didn't like *anybody* the first time he met them.

Max was studying some sort of electrical diagram, and I interrupted his reading to tell him about Dustin Gray and how Nick nearly got beat up at the basketball court. Max's brown eyes widened in surprise. "I wish I had seen that," he whispered.

The stewardess stopped and asked us if we wanted

a snack. I automatically nodded yes to a bag of peanuts. Max shook his head.

"Imagine Nick in a fight!" Max said. "He's so cool, I can't imagine anyone daring to pick a fight with him. That Carmen guy must have really been crazy." Max thought Nick was the next best thing to centrifugal force.

"Maybe." I squinted and looked out the window. "Or maybe it wasn't that big a deal, and this Dustin Gray guy just jumped in and *pretended* to save Nick from a fight. Maybe he just wanted to get to know Nick. After all, Nick is a rich kid, he lives in a big house—"

"Come on, Cassie," Max cut me off impatiently, punching my arm. "Get real. Nobody steps into the middle of a fight just because they want to see the inside of someone else's house. That's illogical."

I shrugged. "I don't know," I answered, scowling. "I just don't like the idea of some goofy goon hanging around Nick all the time. Good grief, he was hard enough to live with before, but if he's into all that macho weight-lifting stuff now, he'll be *impossible.*"

Max just smiled and picked up the electrical diagram he had been studying. "I think it'll be fun to have the guy around," he said. "And you shouldn't judge the guy before you even meet him, Cass." He shot me a grin and waggled his eyebrows. "Who knows? Maybe the guy will be a real dreamboat and you'll fall in love with him."

I snorted. "Fat chance."

2

Mom, Tom, and Steffie were waiting for us at the airport. Steffie looked like she had grown a foot in the three months I'd been gone. She definitely had more hair. She squealed when she saw me and ran into my arms.

Mom hugged Max and then me, and Tom beamed at us. I was surprised how good it was to see Tom—though it seemed a little disloyal to feel that way after just coming from my dad's. But, like it or not, things were different since the divorce, and I guess we had all learned to make the best of it.

"Where's Uncle Jake, Dribbles, and Nick?" I asked as we trooped down to the baggage carousel to claim our luggage. "Can you believe it, Mom? I even missed Nick."

Mom's blue eyes sparkled as she lifted Steffie onto her hip. "You'll probably be yelling at him before

15

dinnertime," she said, smiling. "It'll be good to have things back to normal."

"As normal as a crazy house can be," Tom quipped, slipping his arm comfortably around Max's shoulder. "I didn't know what I was getting into when I married into this family."

"Would you do it differently if you had known?" Mom asked, looking at Tom over Steffie's tousled head.

"Not a chance," Tom answered. He bent to give Mom a kiss right there in the airport, and I closed my eyes and walked on ahead. Their kissing didn't gross me out like it used to, but still, it's really strange to see your mom carrying on like a lovesick teenager. Now if it were me kissing my boyfriend, *that* would be a different story.

Speaking of boyfriends . . . I glanced around, checking out the cute guys at the airport. Maybe that's what I needed—a boyfriend. I'd been away from Canova Cove for nearly the entire summer, and there was no telling how many "guy" opportunities I had missed. I'd have to ask Andrea if there were any likely candidates around.

We piled our luggage into Tom's Mercedes, then the black car whisked us home. When we pulled into our circular driveway, I threw the door open and ran into the house, nearly mowing Uncle Jake down in the foyer. "Where's the fire?" he asked, stopping to give my shoulders a quick hug. "Don't tell me— Chip and Andrea are on their way over and you've got to go fix your face."

"No, I just wanted to see Dribbles," I explained, planting a kiss on his grizzled cheek. "But it's good to see you, too, Uncle Jake."

The familiar scent of Uncle Jake's cigar tickled my nose and I laughed. He never actually smoked the stub of a cigar he carried around between his teeth, but he just wouldn't be Uncle Jake without it. Now the cigar stub was bobbing up and down as Uncle Jake waved his hands and pretended to rant and rave about playing second fiddle to a dog.

I slipped by him as Mom, Tom, Max, and Steffie followed me into the hall. Dribbles, my devoted and darling Chinese pug, was probably upstairs, so I took the stairs two at a time and rushed to my room.

One quick glance around told me Dribbles wasn't there. Then I remembered that Nick was taking care of him while I was away, so I sprinted down the hall to Nick's room, flung open the door . . . and ran straight into Goliath.

I promise, that was my first thought. I felt the guy's belt buckle bruise my chin, and running into him felt like hitting a brick wall at fifty miles an hour. I actually bounced back and landed on the floor (and not gracefully, either). I lay on the floor and closed my eyes in total, complete, absolute embarrassment.

"Good grief, Cassie, control yourself!" I heard Nick's voice shake with laughter above me.

Another deeper voice spoke next. *The giant*, I figured.

"Quiet, Nick, I think she's hurt. Are you OK, Cassie?"

I clenched my teeth and wanted to die. It was bad enough that I'd humiliated myself in front of one of Nick's friends, but this had to be Dustin Gray, the guy my family seemed to be in love with.

I didn't answer him, I just flopped my arm over my eyes and wished the floor would open up and swallow me.

"She's OK, she's just hoping for a little attention," Nick said. I jerked my arm back and opened my eyes, giving him a glare that said, *Why don't you just drop dead where you stand.* Good grief, I couldn't believe I used to think it would be fun to have a big brother!

"I don't want attention," I snapped, pushing myself up into a sitting position. "I want my dog. Where's Dribbles?"

"I take it you're the famous singing sister," the hulk said. "I'm Dustin Gray."

"I know who you are," I snapped again, tossing him a quick glance that I hoped showed how uninterested I was. "What I *don't* know is what happened to my dog." I looked at Nick pointedly.

He just shrugged. "He's probably outside in the yard. Uncle Jake built a little pen for him out back after you left."

"My dog's been outside for three months?" I shrieked. I jumped up to my feet and lit into Nick, waving my hands in his face. "You were supposed to take care of him, not stick him out in a cage! Good grief, Nick, what were you thinking?"

"Yeah, Nick, what were you thinking?" Dustin echoed, and anger flared within me. What was *he* doing, making fun of me? I didn't need this grief.

I turned toward the guy and gave him my steeliest "drop dead" look—but Dustin wasn't looking at me, he was looking at Nick as if he was really concerned about Dribbles. I looked at him, confused, then took a moment to look the guy over.

He sure wasn't what I'd expected. I had heard that he was big and strong, and that much was true. But I'd also expected a face like Arnold Schwarzenegger's, with beady eyes and a hard jaw. It was the darndest thing—this guy had the size of Godzilla—and the

19

soft brown eyes of a basset hound. He had gorgeous brown hair, though it was a little long and shaggy, and when he turned to me and smiled, a dimple actually deepened his left cheek.

Suddenly I felt myself blushing. He looked at me, then wiped his hands awkwardly on his jeans. "Sorry about knocking you down, Cassie," he said, smiling sheepishly. "I didn't do it on purpose."

"It was my fault," I answered immediately. "I should look where I'm going."

I looked up—and I mean *up!*—at him again. He was enormous, but those brown eyes . . . I couldn't get over how soft and sweet they were. He had the appealing expression of a puppy. I sure couldn't figure out how he'd managed to save Nick from a fight. That Carmen somebody-or-other must have only looked at Dustin's muscles, not his face. No one could ever be afraid of those eyes.

"I don't know why you two are yelling at me," Nick said, not even noticing that I had forgotten all about Dribbles. "The dog moped around missing her for days. He didn't want to be with me. He was happier outside where he could chase birds."

"Well," I said, tearing my gaze away from Dustin's eyes and stepping backward toward the door. "I guess I'll go find Dribs."

"Hey, Cass," Nick added, wiping sweat from his

brow. "When we finish our workouts, we're going out for ice cream. Andrea's coming, too, so why don't you come along?"

I tilted my head and studied Nick, not sure I'd heard right. *"Andrea's* coming? Is she coming to see me—or you?"

Nick grinned. "She's been coming to see me for a couple of weeks now. I guess you could say we're going out."

My jaw dropped.

My best friend was dating my brother? I knew Andrea had always thought Nick was cute, but I never dreamed he'd actually want to take her out. Still . . . now that Andrea was mature and beautiful, maybe Nick wouldn't think of all my friends—or me—as little twerps.

"Of course, I'd love to go, but . . . " I hesitated. I *did* want to go and talk to Andrea, and I was dying to watch her and Nick together, but if I went, would I be paired up with the jolly brown-eyed giant?

"No buts," Nick said, standing up. He bent from his knees and hoisted an impressive barbell loaded with weights. "Andrea's coming at four o'clock. Be ready then."

I left his room and wandered downstairs, shaking my head.

Nick was dating Andrea.

Dribbles had become an outdoor dog.

Steffie was walking.

Dustin Gray was huge, but kinda cute.

Life sure had changed a lot in just a few weeks.

3

Andrea and I had a great reunion. There's just something about seeing your best friend again when you've been apart for awhile. After we hugged each other and promised to tell all our latest secrets, we headed toward Nick's Mustang convertible, where the guys were waiting.

Just like old times, I thought happily. Well, sort of. This time Andrea sat up front with Nick, and Dustin and I sat in the backseat. Actually, Dustin *filled* the tiny backseat, and I practically sat in his lap.

When Dustin wasn't looking, Andrea turned around and caught my eye. She nodded toward Dustin, grinned, and raised an eyebrow—her "What-do-you-think?" look. I crinkled my nose and shook my head slightly.

"You're crazy, Cass," she answered aloud, not

caring if the guys heard her. "I think you left all your good sense in Houston."

"Look who's talking about good sense," I teased her. "The girl who's dating *Nick!*"

"He's not so bad," Andrea said, looking at Nick with a big smile on her face. She poked him playfully with her manicured fingernail. "I'm learning to tolerate him, just like he tolerates me. Right, Nick?"

"Right." Nick caught Dustin's eye in the rearview mirror, and they both grinned broadly.

I hate it when guys make girls feel totally left out of the conversation. Of course, I couldn't say anything because Andrea and I had been doing the same thing ourselves. Still, it doesn't seem quite as irritating when you're the one who's leaving the others out.

At the mall I noticed that I wasn't the only one intimidated by Dustin's size. As we walked through the double glass doors to the mall, Dustin held the door open for a gray-haired lady. She took one look at his chest and sprinted past us as if we were about to mug her or something. Three junior high boys who were lounging against the wall outside the movie theaters glanced at Dustin and backed away, watching him cautiously. A mom and her little girl who were walking toward us suddenly veered to one side as we approached.

You'd have thought we had the Terminator walking with us.

We entered Tee Smith's Thirty-Two Flavors, our favorite ice cream store, and looked around. A couple about my parents' age were sitting at the front table. Dustin's shadow fell across the table as we were walking by. Without even looking up, the man pulled on his wife's arm and pushed his chair back so suddenly that it toppled over. "You want this table?" the man asked, smiling nervously at Dustin. "We were just leaving." The man and his wife tossed half-eaten ice cream cones into the garbage and hurried out of the shop.

Even the girl behind the ice cream counter acted terrified. Dustin leaned over the counter and quietly asked if there was an extra charge for toppings. The girl took one look at his massive arms and stammered, "Not for you, sir. What would you like?"

I ordered my favorite—mint chocolate chip ice cream with chocolate sprinkles on top—and my fears were confirmed when Dustin took out his wallet to pay for my ice cream, too. So this *was* a date. Nick probably thought he was really sly, setting up his gullible sister with his new friend. What was I, some kind of reward for Dustin's good deed?

I thanked Dustin for the ice cream and joined Andrea at the table where she was slurping a low-fat yogurt shake. "Isn't Dustin dreamy?" she asked, watching Dustin and Nick as they paid for the ice cream. "He's really sweet, Cassie. I knew you'd love him once you met him."

"I don't love him," I answered. I took a tentative lick from my ice cream cone. "Will he think I like him if I eat all this?" I asked Andrea. "Maybe I should only eat half. That way he won't think I'm too grateful."

"Don't be silly," Andrea rebuked me. "He's a nice guy who wanted to treat you to ice cream, that's all."

"I don't know that he's a nice guy," I said, taking another lick. "In fact, I don't know anything about him at all, except that everyone at my house loves him. And as far as Nick is concerned, he's the world's best physical trainer and bodyguard."

"Well, he did help Nick out that one time," Andrea conceded, "but Nick's no wimp, you know, especially since Dustin's been helping him work out."

"Yeah," I giggled, "I've noticed Nick's even *walking* differently. And those weights in his room! The place is starting to look like a gym." I held my nose. "It even smells like one."

The guys came over then, and we hushed our laughter. I concentrated on eating my ice cream as Dustin, Andrea, and Nick carried on a three-way conversation. "I can't wait for school to start," Andrea said, sipping her shake. "Eleventh grade is supposed to be the best."

"I think being a senior is better," Nick said, running his hand over Andrea's blonde hair. "But don't worry, kiddo, you'll get there soon."

"What grade are you in, Dustin?" I asked, trying to think of *something* to say.

"I'm not," he said, grinning at me. "I graduated last year from Cocoa Beach High. I'm spending the summer at home, then—"

"Tell her what you're going to do," Nick interrupted.

"Go to college?" I asked, hoping I could make a long story short.

"No." Dustin shook his head. "At least, not yet. I'm going to join the army for two years."

"What will you do in the army?" Andrea asked, her eyes wide. "I mean, we're not at war now, so what are you going to do?"

"I'm training to be a wheeled vehicle repairman," Dustin said, his face turning a slight shade of pink. "I like cars, and my recruiter said that would be a good job for me. I'll undergo basic combat training at Fort Jackson, South Carolina, then I'll be sent to the Aberdeen Proving Grounds in Maryland for more training. After that, I'll be stationed at Fort Hood, Texas."

Nick slapped the table in delight. "That's great. You'll be going places and doing things—I wish my dad would let me join up."

I nearly dropped my ice cream cone. I wasn't sure, but something told me Tom had his heart set on Nick's attending Stetson University and getting a law degree, just as he had. I didn't think Tom would be very thrilled if Nick joined the army.

"Don't you want to go to college, Dustin?" I asked. I didn't want to be nosy, but I was curious.

"I'd like to," Dustin said with a shrug, "but my dad left us years ago, and I live with my mom and grandmom. There's no way they can afford to put me through school. We thought the army would be a good way to earn the money for college. My army recruiter said that in just two years I could earn eighteen thousand dollars. Plus, I like the idea of serving my country."

Nick beamed at Dustin like he was the most clever guy in the world. "Isn't that *great?*" he asked. "My man here will get to see the world, train hard, and earn money for college, too. I think that's really smart."

Nick stuffed the rest of his ice cream cone into his mouth. He stood up and swallowed, obviously in a hurry to move on. "What do you girls say to a walk on the beach? It's early yet, so let's head out there."

Andrea jumped up right away and grabbed Nick's hand. I purposely stood up slowly and walked out of the shop *away* from Dustin Gray. He wasn't my boyfriend, and I didn't want him to get the wrong idea.

We were outside the movie theaters when Nick excused himself to use the rest room. Dustin went with him, and Andrea and I sat on a bench outside the theaters to wait.

"Dustin is dreamy," Andrea said, elbowing me in the ribs. "You ought to give him a chance, Cass."

"He's too tall for me," I answered, leaning forward with my chin on my hand. "I couldn't even kiss him without standing on a stepladder."

Andrea giggled. "That'd be funny, wouldn't it? The next time we go out, why don't I bring a stepladder, and let's see what happens?"

"There won't be a next time," I answered. "You and Nick can go out all you like, but I'm not dating this Dustin guy. I'm just here because you're my best friend."

"Quick! Look over there, but don't be obvious," Andrea whispered, gesturing with her head toward the doors to the mall. I ducked and glanced to my right. Two older guys wearing dark leather jackets had just come through the doors. They swaggered slowly in our direction, puffs of smoke trailing from their nostrils like dragons.

Andrea looked straight ahead as if she hadn't noticed them. "Don't they look like something out of a biker movie?" she asked, giggling.

I took another peek at them, then turned to Andrea anxiously. "Andrea, they're coming this way. What do we do?"

"Nothing. Just be cool."

I jiggled my foot nervously as my ears picked up the sound of their heavy boots on the concrete floor. Suddenly a wall of black leather stood in front of us, and Andrea and I slowly raised our heads. The two men were standing right in front of us.

"Hey, baby," one of them said, taking his long brown cigarette out of his mouth. He leered down at Andrea, and I could smell beer on his breath as he exhaled. "Lookin' for some action tonight?"

"No," Andrea answered, sounding more confident than she looked. "I'm waiting for my date."

"That skinny dude there?" the second biker asked, pointing past us toward the theater. I turned to look. Nick was coming out of the theater rest room, and he realized what was happening. He didn't look happy.

"That guy's no problem for me," the first guy said, slapping his grease-stained fist into his palm. "Come with me, honey, and tell that twerp you want a real man."

He grasped Andrea's shoulder, and she tried to wriggle free. "Let me go," she said, her voice quivering. He laughed in response, and I felt my stomach lurch. If this was real and not the worst nightmare of my life, I was going to throw up in about ten seconds.

"What's going on here?" It was Dustin. The two guys jerked their heads up, then stepped back quickly, the greasy guy letting go of Andrea's arm.

"Uh, nothin' man, be cool," the second biker said, waving his hands at Dustin. "We were just passin' time, that's all."

"Pass it somewhere else," Dustin retorted, putting his hands on his hips. The bikers turned and walked away without a backward glance, and waves of thankfulness washed over me. *Thank you, God,* I breathed.

Nick stepped out from behind Dustin and clenched his fists. "It's a good thing you stopped me, Dusty, 'cause I was ready to take them out," he said, glaring at the backs of the retreating bikers. "In two more minutes I would have had them both on the ground."

"Well, it's a good thing we didn't need to do that," Dustin said easily, and he extended his hand to me. "Are you all right, Cassie? You look a little pale."

"I'm fine," I said, my voice cracking. I didn't know what else to do, so I took his hand and stood up. As we followed Nick and Andrea out of the mall, I was amazed that my hand felt so small in Dustin's, sort of helpless and feminine. No boy had ever made me feel that way before. I may not have liked Dustin Gray, but I sure liked the way he made me feel.

4

We drove out to the beach and parked on a little side road under bright streetlights. I knew my mom would have a fit if she thought I was actually parking, so I hopped out of the car. "I really feel like walking," I said, stretching my arms in the cool beach breeze. "Who wants to go for a walk?"

"Andrea and I will walk south," Nick said, getting out of the car and slamming his door. "Why don't you and Dustin walk north? We'll meet you back here in about thirty minutes."

Dustin pulled himself out of the back of the car. "Sounds good," he said, waiting by me. "See you soon."

As Dustin and I walked off in silence, I glanced back. I was a little jealous of the comfortable way Nick and Andrea walked and talked. Nick slipped his arm around Andrea's shoulders casually, and she fit next to him like they were cast from the same mold. Looking at Dustin I sighed. We looked like David and Goliath.

I was nervous about being alone with Dustin, but that faded as we walked and he didn't do or say anything stupid. The steady rhythm of the waves relaxed me a little, and the wind blew my hair into a mass of tangles. I was surprised when Dustin patted my head awkwardly and said, "I like your hair, Cass. It always looks really soft and natural."

I stopped in my tracks. No one had ever told me they liked my hair. Not even Chip. My hair was curly beyond control on its best days, and when I was surrounded with water and wind like I was now, I thought it looked like a big snarl of seaweed.

"Th-thank you," I stammered. "No one's ever told me that before."

"Really?" Dustin seemed genuinely surprised. "I was almost afraid to say anything 'cause I was sure you heard stuff like that all the time. I wouldn't want you to think I was coming on too strong or anything. I know you kind of got suckered into this thing tonight."

"I don't mind being here," I answered, surprised that I really meant it. Except for the scene with the bikers in the mall, the night had been fun. I smiled up at him. "Don't worry, I didn't think you were

34

coming on too strong. And I really appreciate what you did for us back at the mall there. Those guys were . . . well, I was really scared."

Dustin looked out across the water, and a faraway look crossed his face. "It really bothers me when men put those moves on women. I mean, I live with my mom and grandmom. I've seen men bother them, and I've seen the way it makes them feel . . . scared and pushed and angry all at the same time. It makes me boiling mad just to think about it."

I laughed. I didn't think anything could make Dustin "boiling mad." Even at the mall, he had seemed cool as ice.

"You know what I can't stand?" I grinned up at him. "I can't stand it when girls flirt with guys and then act all innocent and surprised when a guy reacts to them. I think that's so phony!"

"I know what you mean. Last year this girl at school did something like that to me. She told everybody that I was puttin' the moves on her, and then when I didn't invite her to the prom, half the school was mad at me. Even the girl I did invite got mad and wouldn't go. So there I was, home alone on prom night, just me and Grandmom. . . ."

We talked forever. At least, it felt that way. I found myself telling Dustin things that I had never told anyone—things about America Now, about my dad, about Chip, about my dream of being a professional singer. I even told him about my belief in God and how I'd given my life to Christ a few years before. Dustin looked at me curiously when I was telling him about this, but he didn't clam up or act embarrassed.

"I've heard of people who did that," he said simply. "But I never understood it. I mean, I believe God and Jesus are real. I think I always have. We used to go to church every Sunday until Mom started working on Sundays. Now we're out of the habit, I guess, but I still pray every now and then."

"When you're in trouble, right?" I asked, laughing.

"Sure," Dustin answered. "Isn't that what everybody does?"

"Not everybody," I said, still smiling. "I mean, I pray sometimes just because I want to talk to God, to tell him what I'm thinking or feeling. You know, because he's my friend." Dustin was looking at me with interest, and I felt my cheeks growing warm. I grinned and reached out to poke one of his muscled arms. "Anyway, I can't believe you're ever in trouble. You look like a guy who can take care of himself."

"I'm usually in all kinds of trouble," Dustin said, but his eyes were smiling. "And Nick will hate us if we don't get back. We've been walking for forty minutes."

We turned and sprinted down the beach until my side ached from running. But when we piled back into the car I discovered something amazing: I didn't hate Dustin Gray anymore. He was huge, but I'd expected that. What I hadn't expected was that he was really sweet.

I glanced at him as I settled into my seat, and his soft, basset-hound eyes met mine. A warmth washed over me, and my eyes widened in surprise. This guy sure could make me feel special.

If only I didn't look like such a peanut next to him.

5

The phone rang early the next morning, and I groggily reached out to pick up the extension in my room. "Hi, Cassie," Dustin said.

I recognized his booming voice right away. "Oh, hi Dustin," I said, trying to hold back a yawn. "I suppose you want me to wake Nick up."

"No, Cassie, I wanted to talk to you."

I couldn't help smiling. I gently scratched Dribbles's ears, wondering what Dustin wanted from me.

"I wondered if you and Nick and Andrea wanted to come over for dinner tonight," he went on. "But of course," he added shyly, "I wanted to ask *you* first before I talked to Nick and Andrea. I didn't want you to get stuck again."

"Dinner? At your house? You talked your mom into cooking for all of us?"

"No, Mom goes to work at four o'clock. But my grandmother will be here."

"You're making your poor grandmother cook?" I teased him. "That's not fair, is it?"

"No, *I'm* cooking," he said, and I sat up in my bed in amazement.

"You cook?"

"Sure. I had to learn when Mom went to work. I'm pretty good. I can promise that I won't poison you or anything."

"*What* are you cooking?"

"That's a surprise. Say you'll come, though, OK? Ask Nick if he'll bring you and Andrea around four o'clock. That way you can actually watch the chef in action."

"OK," I answered slowly. "See you then." I hung up the phone and sat for a moment in silence. Dustin Gray wasn't at all what he seemed. I mean, how many muscle-bound giants could cook? Uncle Jacob cooks at our house and won't even let anyone else in the kitchen, but Uncle Jake was a man—Dustin was a guy, like Nick, and Nick didn't know a spatula from a spoon.

I pulled on my robe and went to tell Nick the news. Whatever happened, it was bound to be an interesting night.

Max actually got Nick to leave the weights for an hour or two to help with Max's latest project. The electrical diagrams he had been studying on the plane were plans to make our house a "smart house" or, as Max called it, "an intelligent environment." With a few appliances and a lot of wire, Max was planning to computerize our house.

"It'll be great," he explained to Mom, Tom, and Uncle Jake in the den. "The central computer system will operate energy-saving heating and air-condition-ing systems, the burglar alarm, the lawn sprinklers, and kitchen appliances. The computer can even be programmed to recognize voice commands."

"Not my voice," Nick interjected, waving his hand. "*I'm* not going to do anything in the kitchen."

"No one's asking you to," Uncle Jake bellowed, glaring at Nick. "The kitchen is my domain, sonny." He nodded at Max. "Go ahead, Maxwell Smart. What else will this system do?"

"We can train a camera on Steffie, so wherever she is, her image will be flashed across the television screens," Max said, looking at Mom. "You won't have to wonder where she is or what she's doing. In addi-tion, the appliances will listen to each other. You can program the microwave from the telephone. You can dial the telephone from the microwave, and turn off the coffee maker from the computer keyboard."

"It all sounds complicated," Tom said, frowning. "And not very useful. I mean, isn't it easier just to

41

turn on the coffeepot instead of entering the computer codes to do it?"

"We can also program the system to automatically lower the volume on the television and radio when the doorbell or telephone rings," Max said. "And after a power outage, a battery-operated master clock will reset all the digital clocks. No more flashing numbers."

"I like that," Mom said, smiling indulgently at Max. "That's practical."

"Motion detectors will switch lights on and off," Max went on. "And a video camera at the front door will switch on when a visitor comes so you'll be able to see who's knocking from any television in the house."

"You can do all this without costing me a fortune?" Tom asked, his left eyebrow rising.

"Yes." Max nodded. "If you'll just let me and Nick try. We're also going to wire the stereo throughout the house, so you can listen to music from any room in the house."

Nick grinned, and Tom shook his head. "My music," Tom said definitely. "Not Nick's music. Nick can still keep his music in his room, on the headphones."

"Deal," Nick said, standing up. "I want to learn

how to do all this stuff. When do we get started, Max?"

Max drew himself up to his full height, which still only brought him to Nick's shoulder. "Right now," he said, and together they trooped off to the garage.

"He's *cooking?*" Nick exclaimed later as the Mustang pulled away from Andrea's house. "I can't believe that. Maybe he meant he would order pizza or something."

"No, he said he was cooking," I answered, annoyed that Nick wouldn't believe me. Obviously he thought Dustin was too manly to know his way around the kitchen. Nick's macho attitude was really beginning to bug me.

Andrea stayed out of the argument. She just smiled at me from the front seat. I had to admit she looked beautiful when she was with Nick. Her eyes were gleaming. "I don't care who cooks," she said brightly, laying her hand on Nick's arm. "I'm starving! I'll eat anything!"

Dustin's house was in a subdivision called Rockledge. It was a group of older Florida houses, all similar and all made from cinder block. The street was cluttered with cars and kids, but Dustin's house, white with deep blue trim, was simple and pretty. I knew before we even went inside that we'd find three bedrooms, two baths, a living room, and a kitchen. My family had lived in a similar house when I was little, before Dad started making more money at NASA.

A late-model Ford sat in the driveway, and Nick parked on the street. "That's Dustin's mother's car," he said, pointing to the Ford. "She'll be leaving for work soon, so I can't block her in."

"They only have one car?" Andrea asked quietly. "How do they manage?"

"They manage," Nick answered with a shrug, pushing his door open. "Now come on, girls. Let's see what Dustin's up to."

We trooped to the front door and rang the bell. A minute later Dustin swung the door open and grinned at us. "Come on in," he said, standing back so we could squeeze by him through the narrow foyer. "Mom's getting ready for work, and then we'll have the kitchen all to ourselves. I figured we could all make dinner together."

"I'm not cooking," Nick protested even as he followed Dustin through the small living room. I tossed my purse on a faded flowered sofa and was surprised to see a thin, gray-haired woman in an upholstered rocker in the corner of the room. She didn't pay any attention to us; her eyes were fastened on the glowing television set in front of her.

"I see your grandma's watching wrestling again," Nick remarked.

"Yeah," Dustin said, pausing for a moment before the woman in the swivel rocker. "Mimi lives for wrestling." Dustin waved his hand and the woman fastened bright, birdlike eyes on him. "Who's wrestling today, Grandma?" he yelled. "Is it the Hulk?"

"Jake the Snake," she answered in a brittle voice. She turned her eyes back to the screen. "He's the best. Go, Jake!"

Andrea giggled, and I pushed her into the kitchen. A round woman with bleached blonde hair stood at the sink, finishing a glass of Coke. Her eyes narrowed when we came into the room.

"Andrea, Cassie, this is my mom," Dustin said. "Madge Gray."

Mrs. Gray was wearing the bright orange uniform of Cash and Carry, a local grocery store. She took a moment to wash her hands before speaking to us. "I know all about you girls," she said, turning back to us as she wiped her hands on a dish towel. She leaned against the counter and pointed at Andrea. "You're the one who went to New York to be a model, right?"

Andrea nodded silently.

The woman pointed at me. "And you're the one who traveled in that politician's singing group. I read all about it in the paper." She folded her arms. "I don't know how my son has fallen into such high and mighty company, but—" She broke off and shrugged.

I had the distinct feeling that Madge Gray didn't like us.

"Well," Mrs. Gray said as she kissed Dustin on the cheek and reached for her purse on the kitchen table, "I'm off to work, so I'll leave you kids here with Grandma. Dustin, make sure she eats, OK? And remember to give her the pink pills after dinner. Two of them."

"OK, Mom," Dustin said. Mrs. Gray gave us one final scrutiny before going out the front door.

One thing was for sure: Dustin didn't get his sweet nature from his mom.

Dustin really did know how to cook. He put Nick to work chopping green bell peppers, and he gave Andrea a huge knife and an onion. "Cassie, why don't you measure out a tablespoon of oil, a teaspoon of chili powder, and a half a teaspoon of garlic powder," he suggested. "You can combine everything in a bowl from that cabinet over your head." Then Dustin took a package of chicken breasts out of the refrigerator and cut them into slices.

Nick got up for a minute to turn on the radio ("It won't bother Grandma," Dustin pointed out. "She's nearly deaf."), and we discovered that cooking was actually fun. We laughed at Andrea, whose eyes ran like faucets while she cut the onion. Dustin told her the fumes wouldn't bother her if she held a slice of bread in her mouth while she chopped. The sight of Andrea with a slice of bread hanging from her lips was hilarious, but she said anything was better than crying off all her mascara. Nick was about to bust his gut laughing.

After the chicken was cut into long strips, Dustin stir-fried the slices in oil, then I stirred in the chili powder, salt, and garlic powder. Nick tossed in Andrea's onion and his green peppers, and Dustin stirred the entire concoction until the vegetables were a little tender.

I was amazed that a guy would know his way around the kitchen, but Dustin definitely did. Next he turned on the oven and had Andrea roll out a can of pizza crust. He gave me a package of Monterey Jack cheese and a shredder, and I shredded cheese while Andrea rolled out the pizza crust.

"What is this we're making?" Andrea asked as she wet her fingers and pushed the sticky dough around on a pizza pan.

"Fajita pizza," Dustin answered, spreading the

chicken and vegetables over the crust. He then spooned salsa sauce over the chicken, then tossed the shredded cheese over the entire creation. It looked great, and after fifteen minutes in the oven, it tasted wonderful!

We gave Mimi a slice, and then ate every bite of the rest. "I guess we should have made two pizzas," Dustin said, pushing his chair back from the table. "I could probably eat one of these by myself."

"Me, too," Nick added.

Andrea and I started to clear the table while Nick and Dustin cleaned the mess in the kitchen. When our dishes were scraped and stacked by the sink, I went into the living room to see if Dustin's grandmother was finished with her dishes.

"Are you finished?" I asked. "Can I take your plate?"

The woman's eyes did not budge from the television screen until there was a break for a commercial. Then she looked up at me and cupped her hand to her ear. "What did you say?" she called. "Who are you, honey?"

"I'm Cassie," I said, stooping down to her level. I raised my voice. "Are you finished with your plate?"

She nodded and pushed the plate toward me. "Are you Dustin's girlfriend?" she yelled.

I looked away, embarrassed. I was sure Dustin had heard her. What should I say?

"I'm his friend and I'm a girl," I yelled back.

"Good," Grandma answered. "You look awful sweet."

6

After dinner we played Pictionary, guys against girls. Andrea and I had an unfair advantage because we've known each other for so long. I could just look at her and make two lines on the paper, and she knew exactly what word I was thinking of. Nick kept complaining that it wasn't fair, but Dustin just laughed good-naturedly and said it wasn't their night to win.

We were nearly through with the game when Andrea drew a totally messed-up picture. "Jesus Christ!" she yelled, furiously scribbling over her drawing. "I can't draw worth anything tonight."

I winced. "Andrea, I wish you wouldn't say that," I said gently. "Jesus Christ isn't a curse word to me. It hurts me to hear his name used like that."

"I wasn't cursing," Andrea answered, pouting. "Honestly, Cassie, you're just too sensitive about things like that. I didn't mean anything by it."

51

"That's the point," I said. "You didn't mean anything, but that name means a lot to me. Just like your name means a lot to me because you're my best friend. I wouldn't like to hear someone using your name that way." I looked down at my lap. More than anything, I wished Jesus meant something to Andrea, too.

"Don't preach, Cassie," Nick said, moving his game piece over the board. "You'll ruin our fun."

"She hasn't ruined anything," Dustin said. I looked up at him gratefully, and his eyes were warm and friendly. "If saying 'Jesus Christ' upsets Cassie, then I'm not going to say it around her."

"Good grief, lighten up," Andrea said, yawning. "Are we here to have fun or what?"

"We *are* having fun," Dustin answered. "I love losing to girls."

He smiled at me from across the table, and I felt my cheeks growing hot.

When it came time to say good night, Nick and Andrea slipped out the front door and I stayed behind in the kitchen to help Dustin finish putting the dinner dishes away. He washed, I dried, and together we made short work of the pile of stuff in the sink.

"Thanks, Cassie, for your help," Dustin said, wiping the counter with a wet cloth. "I really appreciate it."

"Thank you for the invitation," I answered lightly. "It was really fun. I think even Nick had a good time, and he hates to do anything in the kitchen except eat."

Dustin laughed and came close to me. He put his hands on my shoulders and my brain spun like a top—was he going to kiss me? I didn't really want him to . . . or did I? He stared at me and I closed my eyes, too self-conscious to stare back.

He didn't kiss me. Instead he gently tweaked my nose, then turned me toward the front door. "The lovebirds are out there waiting for you," he said, his voice echoing in the quiet house. "See you later, Cass."

I slipped out and cringed as the screen door banged behind me, but then I remembered that Dustin's grandmother was so hard of hearing that the noise wouldn't really matter. The only thing that mattered was that Dustin Gray was wonderful.

Oh, he wasn't for me, of course. But for some lucky girl, he would be wonderful boyfriend material.

7

School was to begin on August 29, one week away. Part of me was looking forward to school; I really wanted to see all my other friends again. But I also dreaded the homework, the studying, and Mom and Tom's school-night curfew.

There was something else I didn't like about August twenty-ninth, too: it was the day Dustin was to report to basic combat training—and I didn't want him to go.

Nick, Andrea, Dustin, and I had been together almost every day since I'd been back from Houston. None of us had much money, so we either hung around our house, swimming in the pool or watching movies on the VCR, or we hung out at the beach. Once Uncle Jacob actually let us use his kitchen, and we made four fajita pizzas for our entire family. Another night Dustin and Nick strapped on tool belts and helped Max string electrical wire under the carpets for our new "smart house."

I thought Nick was a riot, strutting around in his leather tool belt trying to look "manly," but I didn't dare laugh because I would hurt both his and Andrea's feelings. Somehow the tool belt just didn't fit his preppy image. Dustin, though, looked great in anything he wore. You could tell he was all guy. And Max absolutely thought he was the greatest. Dustin treated Max like an equal, not like some weirded-out superbrain. By the end of the evening, they were talking and laughing together like they'd known each other forever. I hadn't ever seen Max click with someone that fast. I couldn't exactly blame him, though. Dustin *was* the greatest.

While Dustin and I were together, we didn't fight or get upset with each other even once. Mom said we reminded her of old married people because we were so comfortable with one another. But as much as I had grown to like Dustin, I still wasn't too sure about being paired up with him. For one thing, school was starting soon, and I didn't want to be going steady with a guy in the army. I mean, if people thought I had a boyfriend, no one else would ask me out the entire year! I envisioned a long string of lonely, dateless Friday and Saturday nights. . . . I didn't want to spend my entire junior year sitting home on the couch! Besides, Mom and Tom had said I could single-date when I was sixteen (come on December!), and I didn't want that freedom to go to waste.

Also (and I felt guilty about even thinking this), I felt really awkward around Dustin because he was so big. Don't get me wrong—he wasn't fat or anything. In fact, his waist was really trim. But he was so muscular and tall that everybody turned to stare at him when he came into a room. I just didn't know if I could get used to being with Schwarzenegger Junior. I knew some girls really went for guys like that, but I'd always found that kind of size a little . . . well, *frightening*.

There was one more reason I wasn't sure I wanted to be Dustin's steady girlfriend. I really didn't think he was a Christian. My youth pastor, Doug Richlett, had always said it was important for Christians to date only other Christians. Of course, I wouldn't call what Dustin and I had been doing so far *serious* dating. We'd been more like a foursome than a couple. Besides, I didn't really understand why Doug felt so strongly about that issue, but I had no doubt that he did. And I respect Doug a lot, so I ended up feeling a little guilty whenever I thought about going steady with Dustin.

The thing was, it would have been *so* easy to fall

in love with Dustin. Too easy. He was kind, gentle, and more like a knight in shining armor than any other guy I'd met. You know that song, "I am a man who will fight for your honor. . . . I'll be the hero you've been dreamin' of. . . ."? Well, Dustin was the guy on the white horse. Whenever I heard that song on the radio I forgot all my reasons for not wanting to go with Dustin and just fell into feelings about living forever with him "for the glory of love."

"Mrs. Dustin Gray. Mrs. Cassiopeia Priscilla Perkins-Gray. Cassie Perkins-Gray." The other day I sat and wrote those names over and over again in my diary, just trying them on for size. We could get married after Dustin's out of the army, in two years. I'd be almost eighteen, and Dustin would be ready for college. Or, if that wasn't practical, we could wait until we both had graduated from college. You know, graduate on Friday, get married on Saturday. We'd have babies—little toddling hunks like Dustin and sweet little pixie girls like me. We'd live in a little house like Dustin's, and Nick and Andrea would live next door; our kids would play together, and Mom and Tom and Dad and Mrs. Gray and even Grandma Mimi would come over to see us all.

Then, every night, after the kids were in bed, I'd curl up in Dustin's strong arms and know that nothing in the world could ever hurt me. No one would ever bother me, and Dustin would never leave me like Dad left Mom. Dustin knew how terrible that was because his dad left, too. We'd promise each other that we would *never* have a fight or get a divorce. Life would be so wonderful! Just us two, living together in the glory of love.

Dustin didn't come around much during the day that last week before school, and I began to think he was avoiding me. On Thursday I finally got up the nerve to ask Nick why Dustin wasn't hanging around as much as usual.

Nick stopped pressing weights long enough to make a sour face. "We were hoping you wouldn't ask," he said, and I felt my heart sink. "Dustin's been working, mowing lawns in his neighborhood. We wanted to take you and Andrea someplace special on Saturday because this is our last weekend together, and Dustin's been trying to raise money."

"Really?" I could have kissed Nick. I bent down closer to him and stuck my finger in his ribs. "Tell me where we're going, or I'll tickle you."

Nick grinned. "Don't tickle me, I'll tell. I told Andrea last night so she could ask her parents. We wanted to take you two to Disney World."

"Yes!" I stood up and clapped my hands together.

"That'll be great! Can we spend the whole day there?"

Nick nodded. "I promised Dad we'd be home by ten, but that will still give us nearly thirteen hours there. Dustin and I figured we'd leave here about eight o'clock Saturday morning."

"Nick, I could just kiss you!"

"Don't," he retorted dryly, gripping his barbell again. "Save that for someone who would appreciate it. Like Dustin."

Even though it was no longer a surprise, I thought Disney World was the greatest idea for a date that I had ever heard. On Saturday morning we piled into Nick's convertible, pulled the top down, and checked our supply of sunscreen. Dustin had a sunburn already, and though I didn't say anything, I knew it was because he'd been outside mowing lawns all week. That was so sweet! No guy had ever worked so hard for me before.

It took us about an hour to reach Mickey Mouse land. The highway was fairly deserted until we neared Orlando, then we followed the line of out-of-state license plates that were headed for Disney World. We had a choice, of course, between MGM, Epcot, or the Magic Kingdom. Andrea and I voted for the Magic Kingdom. The other parks are really cool, but we knew the Magic Kingdom has the most romantic rides.

We parked the car in the section marked Happy (for one of the seven dwarfs), row seventy-nine. We helped Nick raise the top in case one of our sudden Florida showers sprang up, then we were off to catch the tram into the Magic Kingdom. I was so excited I practically skipped through the parking lot. "Slow down," Dustin said, taking my hand. "They'll wait on us."

The day was perfect. I forgot all my reasons for not wanting to like Dustin too much and concentrated on having a good time with him. That was easy. We went through the main gates, where the guys bought our tickets (I understood then why Dustin had had to work so hard—Disney World is not cheap!), and before I knew it we were in that curious, magical world.

"You see those odd doors in some of the buildings?" Andrea asked, pointing to the houses and storefronts on colorful Main Street. "Lots of those go to the underground where the employees work. There's an entire city underneath this place."

"How would you know about that?" Nick asked, a teasing glint in his eyes.

"My cousin works here," Andrea answered, tossing her blonde ponytail defiantly. "He says there's a humongous wardrobe room, a recording studio, a cheap cafeteria, and miles and miles of this tubing that acts like a huge vacuum cleaner for garbage. All the stuff they've got down there is incredible."

"I believe it," Dustin said, looking around. "Well, where do we go first? Tomorrowland and Space Mountain? Frontierland? The Haunted Mansion?"

We consulted our maps and decided to head for Space Mountain before the lines got too long. As we hurried to Tomorrowland, we forgot all about our dignity and ran, holding hands.

As we stood in the long winding line inside Space Mountain, I looked at the darkened roof above me and watched the stars and asteroids whirl overhead. "You see those things that look like planets?" Dustin said, pointing overhead to the images that shone briefly on the ceiling. "Those are chocolate chip cookies. Really. Just look and you'll see."

I waited until one of the planets whirled by again and laughed. "You're right. How funny!"

The line moved up, and I followed the man ahead of me, a young father who was having trouble keeping his three children in line. Suddenly I felt Dustin's strong arms around me, and he gave me an affectionate squeeze. "I'm going to miss you, Cassie," he said, his breath tickling my right ear. "You'll write me, won't you?"

I looked back at him and patted his arms. "Yeah, I'll write," I whispered. "Nick's terrible about writing, so I'll keep you up on everything that's happening in Canova Cove."

"I'd rather read about what's happening with *you*," Dustin said, his breath warm on my ear. "I really don't care much about Canova Cove."

A tingle of pleasure rose from my toes and traveled all the way through me. I didn't know what to say.

The line ahead of me moved again, and Dustin let me go so I could step up. Behind us, Nick and Andrea were arguing about whether or not it was possible for a Fig Newton to look like a space cruiser, but I didn't join in the debate.

I just wanted Dustin to put his arms around me again.

8

We did all that could be done at Disney in one day.
We rode through It's a Small World—only because
Andrea and I wanted to see it. The guys thought it
was boring, but they did it for us (what devotion!).
We went through the Haunted Mansion, sat in on
the Country Bear Vacation Hoedown, and even
climbed through the replica of the Swiss Family Rob-
inson's treehouse. On our way out of the park, we
stepped into the long line for the Pirates of the Caribbean.

I don't know if you've ever been through the
Pirates ride, but the line winds around through several shadowed rooms of a Spanish fortress until you
get into the little boats that take you on the ride.
We talked and laughed for the twenty minutes we
stood in line, and soon we were in the boats. We
rode through the scenes of battle with the pirates,

and as usual, I pointed up to the pirate who sits on top of the bridge that the little boats pass under. The poor guy has hair and mud all over the front of his leg—that's how realistic Disney is—but the back of his leg, which we could barely see—is as clean-shaven as my leg on a good day.

Anyway, Dustin laughed at the hairy-and-smooth leg. Then, while I was looking past him at another display, his hand gently caught my chin and lifted my face, and suddenly his lips were on mine. My first reaction was to sputter in confusion, but I couldn't do that 'cause he was kissing me. So I kissed him back.

The kiss was really nice, soft and sweet, and I forgot all about the pirates of the Caribbean. I should have remembered, though, because there's a waterfall that the boats splash through, and I didn't know we were there until we were halfway through it. Dustin and I were in the front seat, so we got soaked. Nick and Andrea laughed at the sight of our wet faces and clothes, but I didn't care.

We came out of the ride quietly and walked out of the Magic Kingdom without saying a word. Dustin's strong arm held me tight to his side, and I felt like I was going to cry. I really liked Dustin. More than ever. And I hated to think that in two days he'd be gone out of my life for a long, long time.

I linked both my arms around his waist as we walked and buried my head against his side. "You'll forget about me, I know," I said, trying not to cry. "You'll be busy up there in South Carolina or wherever you are, and you'll forget all about me. But I'll never forget about you."

He patted my shoulder gently. "I won't forget about you, Cass," he said softly. "There's nobody like you, not here, and not in South Carolina. I won't ask you to wait for me, because I want you to feel free to date other guys, but please write to me, OK?"

As an answer, I lifted my face to his, and Dustin stooped to kiss me. Behind us, Andrea laughed. "I guess you didn't need a stepladder after all, did you, Cassie!"

I almost overslept and missed church the next morning because I was dead tired and still dreaming about our Disney day—about Dustin's kisses (three of them!), about how secure and content I felt when I was with him. I wasn't sure what love was supposed to be like, but I was pretty sure what I felt was the beginning of it.

I got dressed and joined Max downstairs, where Uncle Jacob waited to drive us to church. Max winked at me from the front seat as we drove. "Did you have a nice time at Disney?" Max asked. "Learn anything new?"

"Hmmm?" I asked, still lost in reverie. "Learn anything? Well, not about Disney, no."

"Ohhhh," Max said, slipping back into his seat. "Learned something about Dustin, did you?"

Uncle Jacob glanced at me in the rearview mirror. "Yup, I saw it coming," he said, tapping the steering wheel with his knuckles. "I can spot true love a mile off."

"Can you?" I asked, scooting forward to look at him intently. "I mean, what *is* true love? How do you know if it's real?"

"Only you can know if it's love," Uncle Jake answered, his eyes smiling at me from the mirror. "And only time will tell if it's true."

I looked out the window. In my life I had loved a friend, been infatuated once or twice, and spent more than my fair share of time with boys—after all, I had two brothers. But none of that seemed to help right now. I still didn't know anything about true love. I wasn't sure I'd know it if it came up and tapped me on the forehead.

Doug stood up in front of our Sunday school class and opened his Bible. "Let's look today at Second Corinthians 6:14-16," he said, flipping through the tissue pages of his Bible. "Follow along as I read:

Do not be yoked together with unbelievers. For what do righteousness and wickedness have in common? Or what fellowship can light have with darkness? . . . What does a believer have in common with an unbeliever? What agreement is there between the temple of God and idols? For we are the temple of the living God. As God has said: 'I will live with them and walk among them, and I will be their God, and they will be my people.' "

I gulped as Doug put down his Bible. This was unreal.

"I want to talk to you today about your dating lives," Doug said, perching on a stool in the front of the room. "Now, I know some of you don't have a boyfriend or girlfriend, and you think you never will. To you, I say, have faith."

Some of the kids in the room snickered, and from the corner of my eye I saw Max lean forward to look at me. I made a face at him and turned back to listen to Doug.

"But school starts tomorrow, and the dating season will begin in full swing. You'll see that cute new girl in school, or that handsome guy, and you'll just be dying to go out with him or her. But before you do, I want you to think about something."

"In Amos 3:3, the prophet asks, 'Do two walk together, unless they have agreed to do so?' What do you think about that?"

A girl I'd seen from time to time spoke up. "I don't know about walking together, but it's a pain to be around someone who disagrees with you. You know, who tries to tell you they're right and you're wrong."

Doug nodded. "You're right, it is a pain. But even if they aren't coming out and telling you you're wrong, how can you build a strong relationship with someone if you don't agree on something as basic as your faith? Suppose you find yourself falling in love with this person—how will you share an understanding love unless your dating partner understands and knows the Savior who guides your life?"

I crossed and uncrossed my legs, feeling uncomfortable. I glanced around the room to see how others were reacting to what Doug was saying, and suddenly I saw Chip. He looked at me and waved. Had he heard that I was dating Dustin?

"So does that mean we shouldn't be friends with someone who isn't a Christian?" one guy asked.

Doug shook his head. "We should be friendly to everyone. I'm not talking about friendships, I'm talking about dating—"

"Yeah, well, I've gone out with some so-called

Christian guys who were pretty rotten," a pretty girl from the back said, rolling her eyes.

Doug smiled at her. "Hey, I'm not going to tell you that kids who say they are Christians are always telling the truth. Sometimes they aren't, and in that case, the Bible tells us that we can judge a tree by its fruit. You know, watch what a person does as well as listen to what he says. But I am going to say that if you're a Christian and you're considering seriously dating a non-Christian, you should think again. Remember, every date is a potential mate. Marriage with the right person is great, one of the best things around; with the wrong person, it's one of the worst. The Bible says we should be equally joined together, which means the right person for a Christian is another Christian."

I couldn't help frowning. Potential mate? Marriage? Good grief, it wasn't like I was engaged to Dustin! Surely God understood that we wouldn't even be dating after tomorrow because he was leaving for the army and I wouldn't see him for months.

So why did I feel so guilty?

Doug went on, but I stopped listening. It wasn't fair for God to ask me to give Dustin up when we wouldn't be dating anymore. Besides, maybe if we stayed together as a couple, Dustin would see Jesus in me and come to love and understand God more.

71

There was nothing wrong with that! I decided that God would just have to understand about Dustin. If I dated any other guys this year, I'd make sure they were Christian guys. Surely God would be happy with that.

9

Mom and Tom had invited Dustin to Sunday dinner, and I knew it would be the last time I would see Dustin before he left for basic training in South Carolina. Max and I hurried out of church to get home in time for dinner, and I was still breathless from rushing around when Dustin rang the doorbell at one o'clock. "I can only stay until four," were the first words out of his mouth when I greeted him, "but I wouldn't miss this for the world."

"Come on in," I said, feeling a little silly, all dressed up and inviting Dustin in as if this were some formal occasion. "Uncle Jacob fixed a big turkey for dinner, so I hope you brought your appetite."

"Always," Dustin said, patting his trim stomach. "I'm never too full or too excited to eat."

Max stepped into the foyer and let out a yell that echoed through the house: "Dustin's here!"

The patter of Harris feet filled the hall as everybody gathered in the dining room.

"'Bout time you got here, man," Nick said, punching Dustin playfully in the shoulder. He raised his eyebrows and pointed to Dustin's tie. "You didn't have to get dressed up for us."

"I think it's nice that Dustin put on a nice shirt and tie," Mom said gently, reminding Nick that maybe his faded Umbro T-shirt wasn't the best choice for a fancy family dinner.

"Sit here, Dustin, next to Cassie," Uncle Jacob directed, nodding his head toward the empty chair next to me. He was carrying a platter with a humongous turkey on it, and he scowled as Nick blocked his way. "Out of my way, Nicky, or I'll drop this blasted bird right on your head."

When we were all seated around the table, we paused and looked to Tom for the blessing. He was uncomfortable for a moment, then bowed his head and mumbled a standard prayer.

"Dustin," Tom said in his lawyer voice when he had finished praying, "we've really grown to know and appreciate you in the last month. We wish you success and happiness as you leave to join the army."

"Hear, hear," Mom said, and she raised her glass of iced tea. We all did the same, toasting Dustin with whatever we were drinking, and he actually blushed.

"Thank you," he said, fidgeting awkwardly in his chair. "But you've all been great. I won't forget you."

"We want you to come and visit us when you're on leave," Mom said, tying a fresh bib around Steffie's neck.

"Don't let them work you too hard in boot camp," Uncle Jacob teased.

"Don't get hit by any friendly fire," Max added.

"And don't flirt with any other girls," I said, kidding him. But in my heart I had this tiny feeling that I really meant it.

Dustin hung his head in an "aw-shucks" expression. "I'll be on my best behavior," he said, smiling at me.

There was an awkward pause, and then Steffie raised her little finger and pointed at the turkey. "Food!" she yelled, leaning forward, and we all laughed.

"That's right, baby, remind us why we're here," Uncle Jacob said, standing up to cut the roasted bird. "I think this drumstick here has Dustin's name on it. What do you say, kid? Can you eat the whole thing?"

"I could eat both of them," Dustin said, holding his plate out. "Just pile 'em on."

After dinner Dustin and I sat on the porch swing at the back of the house and looked out across the pool. I was surprised that everyone else had disappeared to give us privacy, even Nick. I guess they had all figured out that something was going on between me and Dustin, and they were trying to be nice.

I looked around, though, before settling down under Dustin's arm.

"What's wrong?" Dustin said, running his fingers through my frizzled curls. "Afraid of spies?"

"Not people spies," I said. "Electronic spies. Max and Nick have installed electronic eyes all around the house, and I never know when they might be watching."

Dustin laughed. "Let them watch," he said. "We're not doing anything wrong."

We rocked in comfortable silence for a while, then Dustin cleared his throat. "I'll really miss you, Cassie," he said, running his big hand up and down my arm. "You'd better write me a lot."

"Well, at least once a week," I said, smiling demurely. "Just enough to remind you who I am. You're going to be too busy to think about me."

"No I won't."

"Yes you will." I leaned back against his solid arm and let my feet come off the ground. Dustin's legs were long enough to keep us swinging. "You'll go away to see the world and forget to come home except to visit your mom."

"I don't think so." He suddenly stopped rocking the swing, and he bent and kissed me. Our fourth kiss. My heart pounded with all kinds of feelings: thrill at his touch, sorrow because he was going away, and worry—what if Nick and Max were watching us on a television monitor?

By the time Dustin pulled away, I had forgotten about Max and Nick. All I could think of was Dustin. It wasn't fair that I had just found him and was about to lose him. My eyes filled with tears, and the sight of them seemed to surprise Dustin. He held my face in his hand, and his big thumb wiped away a tear that had fallen on my cheek.

He hugged me to his chest. "Oh Cassie," he whispered. "Thanks for being there for me."

I really didn't know what I had done to make him feel so grateful, but I relaxed against him. We rocked like that for nearly half an hour, then it was time for Dustin to go home and spend time with his mother and grandmother. As I waved good-bye from the driveway, I knew it was the last time I would see him for a long, long time.

The next morning I got up, put on my new outfit for school, and packed my lunch—all without feeling the slightest bit of excitement or enthusiasm. Three neat stacks of new notebooks lay on a table near the front door, and I picked up my stack and slipped into Mom's car with Max. My thoughts were a thousand miles away from Astronaut High School. I'd have given my last tube of mascara to be at the airport with Mrs. Gray, saying good-bye to Dustin.

As I slipped into my first-period class, I looked around and decided that three months of maturity had done nothing for the guys in my class. They all looked scrawny and childish. I suppose the fact that I had spent most of the summer singing with college kids in America Now—and that Dustin was bigger than any two of these guys put together—had something to do with how I was reacting. Whatever the reason, I felt too old to be a junior.

By lunchtime I also had decided that my fears about being dateless for the entire year would probably come true—not because I was "taken," but because there was nobody at Astronaut High School I *wanted* to date. No one in the entire school came close to Dustin Gray.

This was going to be a long, boring school year.

One place that wasn't boring, though, was home. World War III broke out that night at supper. We were all about to sit down at the table when Nick marched in, threw a stack of pamphlets down in front of Tom, and announced that after graduation from Princeton Academy he was going to join the army and be a ranger.

"You're what?" Tom yelled, startling Stephanie. Her baby blue eyes widened in fear.

Nick nodded confidently. "I'm going to join the army, like Dustin. I'm going to be a ranger. Dustin could have been a ranger, you know, but he's just not aggressive enough." Nick threw out his puny chest. "I'm aggressive. The army recruiter said I'd be prime material for the army."

"The army's not getting you," Tom said flatly, passing a bowl of steaming mashed potatoes to Mom. "I sure didn't pay all those thousands of dollars for you to go to a prep school so you could join the army." Tom folded his hands calmly. "You're going to an Ivy League school, you'll earn a few degrees, and then you'll practice law. Then maybe you can run for Congress, or even the Senate. But you're not going to join the army unless there's a war and you're drafted."

Tom gave Nick an "Is-that-clear?" look, and Nick's face grew red. He knew better than to argue with his dad, and it was obvious that Tom wasn't going to talk any more about the army. But Nick took a deep breath and asked another question:

"Why is it OK for someone like Dustin and not OK for me? Do you think we're better than Dustin's family? Isn't that kind of snobbish?"

Tom set his jaw. "No, we're not better than Dustin's family. But Dustin doesn't have a choice, and you do. For Dustin, the army is a good decision. The best decision you can make is to obey your father and continue with your education." Tom raised an eyebrow. "I hope we have ended this discussion."

Nick turned and stormed out of the room, and I breathed a sigh of relief. "I guess he's not hungry," I said, sitting down at my place.

"I guess not," Max answered, his eyes wide.

"What's a ranger?" Mom asked, passing a bowl of green beans.

"Something like the green berets," Uncle Jacob answered. "An elite corps."

"Well, at least Nick aims to be the best," Max said, smiling at Tom. "That's good, isn't it?"

"Not good enough," Tom answered, glaring at the food on his plate as if it were rotten or something. "Not for my son." He picked up his fork and stabbed a slice of leftover turkey. "Now let's drop the subject and eat."

The first letter, written in Dustin's bold block printing, came on Wednesday. He had written it on the plane and mailed it as soon as he arrived in South Carolina.

August 29
Dear Cassie:

Greetings from thirty thousand feet! I miss you already, but I'm excited about beginning basic training. Eight weeks and I'm outta here! I'm looking forward to graduation already! The ceremony will be October 22—Do you think there's a chance you and Nick could come up? My mom and grandmom are coming up on the bus, and you could come with them. There's lots of time for you to let me know. I'd love it.

I guess there's not a lot to say now, but I found this poem by Robert Herrick that I wanted to share with you. It says everything I felt yesterday when we said good-bye.

Why dost thou wound and break my heart,
As if we should forever part?
Hast thou not heard an oath from me,
After a day, or two, or three,
I would come back and live with thee?
Take, if thou dost distrust that vow,
This second protestation now.

Upon thy cheek that spangled tear,
Which sits as dew of roses there:
That tear shall scarce be dried before
I'll kiss the threshold of thy door.
Then weep not sweet; but this much know,
I'm half return'd before I go.

Love always,
Dustin

After reading his letter, I didn't know whether to laugh or cry. It was a beautiful letter, a precious poem, but it was just so different and so—serious! Did he really mean it when he said he wanted to come back and live with me? Did Dustin think we would get *married?* The tiny voice in the back of my conscience pricked me—I'd been telling myself that Dustin and I weren't serious, that we weren't thinking about marriage. Yet, here was this letter. . . .

Andrea stopped by later that afternoon and I showed her the poem. As I expected, she thought it was wonderfully romantic. "You're so lucky," she said, holding the letter to her heart. "What I would give if Nick would write me something like this! Dustin is really a romantic, Cassie. Some girls would kill to have a boyfriend like that."

"I know," I said, taking the letter and refolding it

into its envelope. "He is really sweet, but I don't know how to answer him. I can't write letters like this."

"Just what were you planning to write him?"

"News bulletins and gossip," I answered lightly. "But if I don't write back something at least a little mushy, I'm afraid I'll hurt his feelings. I really like him, Andrea, but I'm afraid of getting too serious. I just don't know what's going to happen."

Andrea shrugged. "Make the soldier happy. Give the guy something to show to his buddies. You don't have to *mean* everything you say. After all, the guy won't be back here for months, right?"

"Probably." I wondered if Andrea was right. It wouldn't hurt to write Dustin a couple of romantic letters, would it? It would make him feel good, and it would keep us close. Besides, how serious could we get with him thousands of miles away?

"OK, I'll write him a slightly mushy letter," I said, pulling a box of stationery from my desk drawer.

Andrea's eyes glowed. "Can I help?"

"No," I answered, pulling the cap off my pen. "I have to do this my way."

10

September 5
Dear Dustin:

I was surprised to hear from you so soon, but I'm glad you made it to camp safely. How's the army treating you? Do you stay in one of those huge barracks like I see on television? Do you have a mean drill sergeant who yells at you all the time?

I was going to write you a really mushy letter, but I can't lie to you. I can only tell you the truth, and the truth is that I'm all confused. I really like you, Dustin, and I really miss you (Nick does, too, but for different reasons). I'm just not sure where time will take our relationship. I guess we have a lot of time to think about it, though.

The poem you sent was really beautiful. I loved it, and I showed it to Andrea (hope you don't mind!) and she loved it, too. I write poetry sometimes in my journal, and I tried to write one for you. Of course, it's not as good as the poem you sent me (and it doesn't rhyme!), but it'll have to do. I wrote it while thinking of you.

THINGS I LOVE
I love roses, soft and budding.
I love music, relaxing and tender.
I love words, expressing an author's hidden world.
I love friends, and having a good time.
I love rain, masterful and gray.
I love storms; they make me feel small.
I love warmth of a home, a hand, a life.
I love eyes; they show the inner soul.
I love God, who gave life to me.
I love rhythms, exciting and captivating.
I love birds, so high and graceful.
I love laughter, the universal language.
I love life and living it minute-by-minute.
I love your smile, the dearest thing I know.

Always,
Cassie

I didn't hear from Dustin for a week. But one afternoon a letter from Dustin arrived for Nick. I waited impatiently until I heard Nick's car door slam in the driveway. A minute later I heard him bounding upstairs, then the door to his room slammed shut. I was dying to know what Dustin had written to Nick, so I picked up the letter and knocked on Nick's door. I could hear him inside, panting. Was he lifting weights *again?*

"Who is it?" he barked.

"Cass. You've got a letter." I didn't wait for the OK, but just pushed the door open. Nick was lying on his weight bench with barbells in his hand. His face was red with exertion, and his left eye was bruised and swollen shut.

"Nick!" I squeaked, "what happened?"

"Come in and shut the door," he whispered, his voice intense. He rested the barbell on his chest. "I don't want Mom and Dad to see me like this. I'm not coming down to supper, either, so just tell them I picked up a burger, OK?"

I walked closer and peered at his eye. "Who did this to you?"

"A guy at school," Nick said. "It's no big deal, no one caught us, or I'd be suspended for sure. I was just razzing him a little bit, and then he hauled off and punched me. My face looks worse than it is." He tried to grin, but grimaced instead. "I got in a couple of good licks myself."

"I can't believe you were fighting." I sank onto the edge of Nick's bed. "What's gotten into you lately? You never used to pull all this macho garbage."

"I used to be a wimp, too," Nick said, hoisting the barbell above his head. "But Dustin showed me that you have to pump up and stand up for yourself. If you're big, nobody will mess with you."

Nick's fascination with muscles had gone farther than I thought it had. "Dustin tried to stop you from fighting," I said, shaking my head. "Dustin's a big teddy bear; he never picked on anybody."

"Being big talks," Nick insisted, clenching his teeth as he pumped the barbell up and down. "And I'm never going to settle for scrawny again."

"Is that why you want to join the army?" I asked. "You think that being a tough, macho soldier will somehow make you more of a man? It doesn't work that way, Nick."

"What do you know about it?" Nick said, glaring at me with his good eye. "You don't know how it feels to stand on the basketball court and have some dude punch you in the chest. To have him call you names while you know that you're at his mercy just because he's stronger and bigger. . . ."

Nick trailed off and pumped harder, and I tossed

his letter onto the floor under his workout bench. "There's your letter from Dustin," I said, standing up to leave. "Read it carefully, Nick. If I know Dustin, there's not one word in there about the fun he's having learning to kill people. You've got this whole thing all mixed up."

"Will you bring me some ice for my eye?" Nick said. "I can't go downstairs without Mom or Dad seeing me."

"No," I answered, opening the door. "If you're such a tough guy, you can face them and get it yourself."

11

September 15
Dear Cassie:

Greetings from hot, sweaty Fort Jackson,
home of army food and the toughest drill ser-
geants on the face of the planet. I'll tell you
what, when I fall out of bed at four-thirty every
morning, I know I have to rise, but the last
thing I'm going to do is shine! We have lights
out at nine-thirty every night, and believe me,
we're all asleep in five minutes. Learning to be
a United States soldier is hard work, but I guess
it's worth it.

I'm sorry I haven't written more often, but
Don Jackson, one of my roommates, gave me a
book to read in my free time, and I can't put it
down. It's about Universalism—ever hear of

that? Anyway, since I knew you were interested in God and things like that, I started to read this book, and it really makes sense. The writer says that Jesus, Buddha, Muhammad, and all the great prophets of the past point to the same God. God is so great, he is giving us thousands of ways to turn to him. What reaches one person may not reach another, so God has given us lots of chances. I like that idea.

Don really knows about this stuff, and on nights when we can stay awake, we talk a lot about life and God. Don says God is more like a universal law than a person, not male or female. And he says that mankind is part of God, therefore man isn't all bad. That makes sense to me. After all, I know lots of good people who don't go to church. Anyway, to make a long story short, I think I'm learning a lot about God here, and I know that would please you. So say hi to your folks for me and stay sweet, OK? I miss you a lot.

Love,
Dustin

P.S. If you have a chance, why don't you drop by and see my mom and grandmom? I know

they'd like to see you again. I write them about
you all the time.

I frowned as I put down Dustin's letter. I was glad
he was interested in God, but all that stuff he was
learning from his roommate didn't sound right to
me. In fact, it sounded downright weird. I stuck his
letter into my Bible and decided to talk to my youth
pastor about it the next time I went to church.

As for going to see Dustin's family, I liked the idea.
Nick would take me there, I knew, and it would be
romantic to be with the other two women who loved
Dustin. Maybe I could take them something. . . . I
snapped my fingers and ran downstairs to ask Uncle
Jacob if I could bake a batch of chocolate chip cookies.
Everybody likes chocolate chip cookies.

I nervously balanced the tray of cookies in my left
hand while I rang the doorbell. Nick sat in the car by
the curb, impatiently tapping his door. "Don't take
forever," he had said as I got out. "I've got places to
go and things to do. Andrea's expecting me."

Mrs. Gray seemed startled to see me. "Uh, hello,
Cassie," she said, opening the front door. "What can
we do for you?"

"I just stopped by to say hello and bring you some
goodies," I answered, handing the tray to her.

"How nice. Won't you . . . come in?" She was polite, but her smile seemed forced, and I had the feeling Mrs. Gray didn't like me any better now than she had when she first met me.

"Sure, but just for a moment," I said, walking by her into the living room. "I promised Dustin I'd drop by and say hello to you and Mimi."

The swivel rocker by the television turned in my direction, and I heard the raspy voice of Dustin's grandmother: "Is that Dustin's girlfriend?"

"It's Cassie, Mother," Mrs. Gray called loudly. "She dropped by to say hello."

"Tell her to come here, then."

I walked slowly toward the television and noticed that Mimi had forsaken television wrestling for a soap opera. She grinned wickedly when she saw me looking at the screen. "I know I shouldn't watch this foolishness," she said, her eyes sparkling, "but I just can't get through the day without my programs. Sit down here, honey, and let's talk a while."

"I'll leave you two because I have to get ready for work," Mrs. Gray said, taking the cookies into the kitchen. "I'll be late if I'm not careful."

As I sat down on the brown vinyl footstool by the rocker, Mimi winked at me and pointed a bony finger toward the kitchen. "She's afraid you'll steal her

baby boy away," she whispered gruffly. "You're
Dusty's first girlfriend, you know."

"No, I didn't know," I said, the vinyl cracking
under me as I shifted my weight. "I thought he'd
had lots of girlfriends."

"What?"

I spoke louder. "I thought he had lots of
girlfriends!"

Grandma shook her head. "No, Dusty's always
been shy around the girls. A real good-lookin' boy,
but shy. He takes after his grandfather. My husband
took nearly two years to propose to me, and he did
it in the buggy while my father sat in the seat
behind us!" She cackled at the memory, and I
laughed with her. This lady was a riot.

"Do me a favor, honey."

"What?"

"Go into Dusty's room there," she pointed at the
first door down the hall, "and bring me the picture
on his dresser."

I paused for a minute, and she waved her hand at
me. "Scoot!"

There was no disobeying Mimi, so I stepped down
the narrow hall and into Dustin's small room. A
twin bed was pushed against the wall, and a battered
dresser stood against the opposite wall. There was
only one picture frame on the dresser, and I picked

it up without glancing at it, but I paused to look around. You can tell a lot about a person from where he lives. Dustin's room was crowded with the things he loved best: a pile of battered barbells in the corner, a bookcase of wooden planks and bricks sagging against the third wall, and a closet bulging with T-shirts and sweatpants. There were two football trophies on the bookcase, a football scribbled with autographs on the bed, and next to his bed was a stained book: *Best Loved Poems by Seventeenth Century Authors.*

Before I'd gotten to know Dustin, I would have been surprised by that book. Now I understood that the soul of a poet lived in Dustin's bruiser body, and that was just one fascinating thing about him. I sighed—I was taking too long—then turned and took the picture to Mimi.

Mimi examined the picture closely, and I looked over her shoulder. The black-and-white photograph looked like a family portrait: a man, a woman, a little boy, and a little girl. I didn't recognize any of them.

Mimi tapped the glass above the little girl's sweet face. "This was April, Dusty's little sister," she said, her finger still tapping on the glass. "She drowned about a year after this picture was taken. She and Dusty were out playing hide-and-seek, and she fell into the pond behind the house. Dusty didn't find her until it was too late."

I groaned and sank onto the footstool at her feet. How terrible!

"Dusty was seven then," Grandma went on, her gaze shifting to the wide smile of the boy in the photograph. "It was after April died that John left the family, and I came to take his place. It's been the three of us ever since."

Her hand began to shake as she held the photograph, and I caught the frame quickly so it wouldn't fall. She looked at me, expecting me to say something. "Thank you for telling me," I stammered. "That helps me to understand Dustin better."

"He's a good boy," she said, giving me the picture and lowering her quivering hand into her lap. "A lot of people don't understand what a good boy he is."

"I do," I answered. I got up and returned the picture to Dustin's room, and realized that hot tears were stinging my eyes. Poor Dustin! How terrible he must have felt! Knowing Dustin, I was sure he must have felt responsible. Had he blamed himself all these years for his sister's death? Did he even think he was responsible for his dad's leaving?

Mrs. Gray was standing by the front door when I came out of Dustin's room. "I've got to go to work now," she said, her voice firm. "But thanks for bringing the cookies. I know we'll enjoy them."

Her tone of voice told me that I should go, but I took a moment to place my hand on Mimi's before I went to the door. "I enjoyed our talk," I said loudly. "I'll come see you again, OK?"

"OK, honey," she said, smiling up at me. As I left the house, I heard her turn up the volume on her soap opera.

12

It's one thing to love somebody because they're wonderful; it's something else to love somebody because they need you and love you, too. I had known Dustin was wonderful for some time, but after learning more about his family, I began to understand why Dustin was so devoted to his mother, his grandmother, and me. In a sense, we were all he had. His father was gone, his sister had died, and his friends (even Nick!) didn't write him very often. He must have felt so alone. But he wrote me wonderful letters every couple of days, and he always thanked me for writing back and "being there" for him.

With every day that passed, I felt myself falling deeper in love with Dustin Gray. I knew I was young, but Romeo and Juliet were young when they fell in love, too. And my mom met my father when she was sixteen. So I knew I wasn't too young to really fall in love. I mean, what is love, really? It's a feeling, a kind of desire to treat someone special, an urge to understand and protect and guard them. I felt all of that and more for Dustin.

Before long, I stopped signing my letters "Always, Cassie" and started writing, "With all my love." I meant it, too. School was a drag, and Tom and Nick had been fighting a lot lately, so life wasn't exactly great—but in Dustin's letters I could lose myself and dream about our little house with the rosebushes in front. Mom and Tom could have their kids and their big house and the mortgage. Dustin and I would have the perfect marriage with adorable kids and a sweet little house. Maybe he'd stay in the army for a while, and we could live on the base and travel all over the world. It would be perfect. Our wedding would be one of those military ceremonies where we'd walk through an arch of upraised swords held by all the groomsmen, who would, of course, be in uniform. It would be outstanding!

One afternoon in study hall I had just finished writing another poem for Dustin when Chip came over and sat down next to me. I looked at him in surprise. There was a time when I wouldn't have gone through a day without at least talking with Chip. Now I hardly ever saw him.

"I hear you're planning to go to South Carolina to

visit your new boyfriend," he said, his blue eyes light and teasing. "So are you serious about this guy or what?"

"Serious enough," I said lightly, quickly folding my poem so Chip wouldn't read it over my shoulder. "Dustin is great."

"So are you going steady?"

I wondered why he was asking, but I shrugged. "We really like each other, but we don't put limits on each other's freedom," I answered. "Dustin said that wouldn't be fair. He didn't want me to sit at home all year while he's in training."

"Oh, and he wanted to date the women on the base," Chip replied with a grin.

"He doesn't have time for a social life," I retorted. "But I wouldn't care if he did date other girls. No one else understands him like I do."

"Ohhhh," Chip said, easing back in his chair. "Excuse me. I didn't know you had a telepathic connection."

"We're very close," I answered, snapping my notebook shut. I was relieved when the bell rang. I gathered my books and prepared to sprint out the door.

"Does that mean you don't want to go with me to the Amy Grant concert next month?" Chip called. "I've got great tickets."

I paused. I really did love Amy Grant, and Chip

was a good friend, too. What harm would it do? But if Dustin heard about it, it might hurt his feelings, and I would never want to do that.

"No, thanks," I said, turning back to Chip. I gave him a genuine smile. "I've got to talk my mom into letting me ride a bus to South Carolina. That'll probably take me all month."

He nodded, looking at me kind of curiously. As I turned and walked away, I felt a twinge of sadness. Loving Dustin was great—but I wondered if it would end up costing me Chip's friendship.

At first Mom said no to my going to South Carolina. Then she and Tom talked about it and decided that since I was going with Mrs. Gray and Dustin's grandmother, I couldn't get into too much trouble. Plus, I'd only see Dustin for a few minutes, because in less than one hour after graduation, he would have to board a transport plane for the Aberdeen Proving Grounds in Maryland, where he'd go through his advanced individual training.

Mom and Tom finally agreed that if Nick and I earned half our money for the bus tickets, we could go. I ran to my room, emptied my secret bank, and found forty-two dollars. Yea! With only two or three baby-sitting jobs, I'd have enough for the trip.

Nick would have to work harder, and I think Mom and Tom were hoping he wouldn't find the money because they didn't want him spending too much time around army people. Nick hadn't actually mentioned joining the army again, but I knew from the way he strutted around the house that he envisioned himself as a green beret or something.

Nick's personality had done a complete turn-around in the last few weeks. Now his favorite movies were war flicks, and he and Max spent hours in the den watching Rambo, Chuck Norris, and even John Wayne—I'd heard them all blasting away in there. The more gunfire in the movie, the more Nick liked it.

I wrote Dustin that we were definitely coming to his graduation, and when I got his reply I couldn't wait to tear open the letter.

October 2
Dear Cassie:

My roommate, Don, remarked that you must love me an awful lot to ride for over fourteen hours on a bus just to see me for half an hour. I guess you do, huh? Well, honey, I love you, too. There's no one in the world like you, girl, and I can't wait to see you, even if it's for only fifteen minutes! I'm living for those moments when I can be with you, feel your hair, and see your big brown eyes. All the grief I've undergone here will be worth it!

I stopped reading and clutched the letter to my heart. Red Letter Day! October 8, at 3:33 P.M. The first time Dustin wrote that he loved me! *He loves me, he loves me!* I closed my eyes and smiled, as a hundred little nagging worries left my heart. He really loved me! Dustin wouldn't say it if he didn't mean it.

After a few minutes, I calmed down enough to keep reading:

I've learned that as soon as I graduate from my AIT at Aberdeen, I'm going to be assigned to the Thirteenth Coscom Unit at Fort Hood, Texas. We support the First Cavalry Division and Second Armored Division, who were recently deployed to Madagascar. Do you know anything about Madagascar? I don't, but I suspect it's been in the news lately. Check out the newspaper—or better yet, have your genius little brother read up and report back to you. We don't get much news around here that hasn't been through the army censor.

Well, sweetie, it's time for me to hit the sack.
Take care, write soon, and I'll see you in twenty
days!

Love,
Dustin

I wasn't sure what happened when soldiers were
"deployed," so I ran to ask Max the Brain. Max said
Congress had recently authorized the deployment,
that is, the transfer, of several thousand troops to
Madagascar.

"Where's Madagascar? *What's* Madagascar?" I
asked, plopping down on Max's bed as he tapped his
computer keyboard.

"Just a minute," Max said, and suddenly a colorful
map of Africa emerged on his computer screen. Max
pointed to a large oblong island off the eastern coast of
Southern Africa. "That's Madagascar," Max said proudly.
"An independent republic with a strong president.
Made up of six provinces, the chief crops are coffee,
cloves, vanilla, rice, sugar, tobacco, and peanuts. They
have one television per every eighty-nine people."

"So?" I crinkled my nose. "Why is our army over
there?"

"Not to fight a war," Max said, tapping on his
computer again. "The president of Madagascar is

probably using our troops as a show of strength. Maybe he perceives a threat from another country, or a rival political party. Our troops probably won't do anything but stand there and look strong."

I mulled over this new information. "Do you think Dustin will have to go there?" I whispered.

Max shrugged. "It depends on the current political climate. Madagascar had a coup in 1973, when the new regime nationalized French-owned financial interests, closed French bases and a U.S. space tracking station, and obtained Chinese aid. The government conducted a program of arrests and deported all foreigners. In 1990, though, they ended a ban on multiparty politics. Now that there's more than one political party, perhaps the president is getting nervous." I looked at Max and shook my head. He could sound like such a little encyclopedia sometimes.

Max drummed his fingers on his desk thoughtfully. "It does seem strange that they would call on the United States for help."

"As long as nobody's getting hurt, Dustin will be OK, won't he?" I asked.

"Don't worry," Max said, switching his computer off. "Who is going to shoot a wheeled vehicle repairman?"

"He's not just a wheeled vehicle repairman," I huffed. "He's a wheeled vehicle repairman who loves me."

106

13

October 21 finally came, and we boarded the Greyhound bus at our little station in Canova Cove and settled in for the long ride to South Carolina. Mrs. Gray sat with her mother, and Nick and I took seats across the aisle from them. Nick took the window seat, so I was stuck in the seat right across from Mrs. Gray, which didn't really thrill me. She still didn't talk to me unless she absolutely had to. I was almost sure she would rather make the trip without me.

I had packed a little overnight bag with two changes of clothes—a dress for the graduation ceremony and fresh jeans and a shirt for the ride home. Our plan was simple: we were going to the army base, we'd watch graduation, maybe eat lunch with Dustin, and then come back home. We'd be spending over twenty-eight hours in a bus, but I didn't care. To see Dustin again, I'd have ridden on the bus for *days*.

It was late afternoon when we left Canova Cove, and Nick and I waited until dark to eat the sandwiches Uncle Jacob had packed for us. The drone of the bus engine lulled me to sleep after we ate, even though we stopped about every twenty minutes in little towns all the way up the coast of Florida and Georgia. When I woke up again, at ten o'clock by my watch, it was dark. Nick was asleep, and so were Mrs. Gray and her mother, so I bundled my sweater into a ball and tried to get comfortable in the seat. I'd probably look terrible when we pulled into Fort Jackson, but I didn't think Dustin would mind.

The next morning Nick got off at one of the small-town stops to get us some breakfast. I curled up in the empty space in his seat and was half asleep when Mrs. Gray's ragged whisper jolted me awake.

"I just think it's silly that she came along," she was telling Mimi. "Imagine, that girl with our son! He has absolutely nothing in common with those people. He's just going to get hurt, Mother, you wait and see. The first time some rich guy comes along, that Cassie will be out of Dustin's life faster than you can change a channel."

I felt the heat rise in my face, and my heart was beating like crazy. What had I ever done to Mrs. Gray to make her feel that way about me? I sat up and cleared my throat. "Excuse me, Mrs. Gray," I said, looking her right in her cold eyes. "I'm not after some rich guy, and I don't want to hurt Dustin. I love him."

Mrs. Gray laughed harshly and threw her hand into the air. She didn't act at all embarrassed that I'd overheard her—in fact, I'd be willing to bet that she was hoping I had. "She loves him," she said to Mimi mockingly, ignoring me. "More than me, probably. Who cares if I'm the one who brought him into the world." She snorted in disgust. "What do kids know about love? Nothing. Absolutely nothing."

She looked at me then, and her eyes glittered with some emotion I didn't know how to read. "Love isn't easy, Cassie," she said, raising her chin proudly. "You'll learn what it really is when things get rough. My husband couldn't handle the rough times, and he walked out. But I never deserted my son, no matter how tough things got. And believe me," she said as her eyes narrowed, "they got tough. Tougher than you've ever had to face with your nice big house and your nice rich family, that's for sure."

"Madge, don't," Mimi said, reaching out and putting a frail hand on her daughter's arm. Mrs. Gray just shrugged her off, still looking at me with those cold eyes. "I stuck it out, Cassie. That's love. Real love. And you don't know anything about that kind of love."

I stared at her for a few seconds, struggling with the desire to throw something at her. *God, help!* I prayed, then leaned back in my seat. Mrs. Gray snorted again, and I could tell she thought she'd won. I turned back to look at her—and saw the anger and pain in her eyes—and suddenly I wasn't mad anymore.

"You're right," I said quietly. "I don't know about what you've faced. But I've been through some crummy things, too, Mrs. Gray. I know what it's like to have someone walk out—my dad did that a few years ago. And I know what it's like to wish things could be different, like they used to be . . . but they'll never be that way again. I know how it feels to lose someone you love, Mrs. Gray. And I wouldn't do that to Dustin."

Before she could answer, I sat back again, leaning against the seat back. Just then Nick came back onto the bus with a couple of gooey cheese danishes and orange juice. I slid over to the window seat and let him sit on the aisle next to Mrs. Gray. He could ride the rest of the way next to her.

A lump rose in my throat, probably anger and frustration because I couldn't seem to get along with Mrs. Gray no matter what I did. I pretended nothing was wrong, though, and bit into the lukewarm danish, thanking God that Nick had come with me. It was awkward enough with the four of us, but if I had been alone with Dustin's family, I'd have probably gone nuts.

Fort Jackson was on the regular bus route, and my legs felt like rubber when we finally stepped out and blinked in the bright sunshine. We had timed it perfectly. It was ten-thirty, and the graduation ceremony was to take place at eleven o'clock. Nick went inside the nearest building to ask for directions to the grandstands, where we could watch the graduation.

As we took our place in the bleachers, I saw a platoon of soldiers lining up far away down the field. They all wore sharp uniforms and caps, and there was no way to tell which of them was Dustin. Nearly all the guys were big and trim, so for once in his life, Dustin didn't stand out.

The company of soldiers advanced as the band played, all proudly stepping together in rhythm. Soon they stood before a colonel, who gave them a snappy salute, which they returned. They stopped marching, were instructed to hold up their hands and repeat an oath, which they did, then suddenly they were cheering and beating each other on the back. My Dustin was now a graduate, a soldier.

Mrs. Gray stood up, and I jumped up with her, scanning the crowd of uniforms. Suddenly I saw him, grinning in our direction. "There he is," I squealed, scampering out of the stands. "Dustin!"

Fortunately, I could run faster than Mrs. Gray. I skimmed across the grass and threw myself into the familiar strength of his arms. "Cassie, it's so good to see you," Dustin whispered in my ear, and I found myself blinking back tears.

Good grief, I hadn't expected to feel this way!

I backed away, about to blubber all over both of us, and Mrs. Gray grabbed Dustin's shoulders and hugged him. Nick brought Mimi up next, and Dustin hugged her, too. Then he and Nick smirked at each other and gave each other high fives.

"You look good, man," Nick said, punching Dustin in the arm. "Even though they did cut all your hair off."

"It'll grow," I said defensively. "And he looks great like this."

"You look good, too, man," Dustin said to Nick. "Still working out, huh? It shows, it really does."

Nick threw his chest out and strutted around like a windup toy, but for once I didn't care what he did. All I wanted to do was hug Dustin! That was impossible now, though, 'cause his mother had one arm and his grandmother had the other.

"My plane leaves at thirteen hundred hours," Dustin said, smiling at us. "That's one o'clock, Mom. So we've got about an hour to go somewhere and talk. There's a little coffee shop over here, if that's OK with everyone."

"Great," Mrs. Gray said, still clinging to Dustin's arm. "Walk slowly though, honey. Don't forget your grandma can't run around like you young 'uns."

The three of them led the way to the coffee shop, and Nick and I followed behind in their shadows. Somehow this reunion wasn't quite what I had expected.

"Son, you look real thin," Mrs. Gray told Dustin after we had settled into a booth in the coffee shop. "Aren't they feeding you enough?"

"They feed us plenty," Dustin said, grinning at Nick, who sat across the table next to Mrs. Gray. Mimi and I were squeezed into the seat with Dustin. At least Mimi had the good sense to slide into the booth first so I could sit next to my boyfriend.

"What will you do in Maryland?" Nick asked, his eyes bright and eager.

Dustin shrugged. "Mainly learn about vehicles. Basic training was for combat readiness, I guess, and so we'll get used to the army way. Now I've got to learn to do my job. After fifteen weeks of training, I'll be MOS qualified—"

"M-O-what?" Nick said, looking at him curiously.

"'Military Occupational Specialty,' my job. Once I'm MOS qualified I can go anywhere in the world."

Dustin's voice was proud, but his words sent a shiver up my spine. Go anywhere in the world? That meant he could be sent overseas, to a big war like Vietnam, or even a little war like Grenada. I didn't want him to go anywhere, and I grabbed his arm firmly. I wanted him to stay here forever, right next to me.

"I wanted to meet your sergeant," Mrs. Gray fumed, fussing with her napkin.

"Don't sweat it, Mom," Dustin said agreeably. The waitress approached the table and looked at Dustin. "Are you ready to order here, soldier?"

Mrs. Gray waved her napkin. "I'll have coffee and a BLT, please, and my mother will have the same. My son will have scrambled eggs and toast, and—" she peered past the waitress at the baked goods displayed on the counter. "Do you have fresh-baked muffins? Dusty loves fresh baked muffins."

"I can order for myself, Mom," Dustin inserted, and I thought he seemed a little edgy.

The waitress looked at him, one eyebrow raised, and Dustin flipped the menu toward her. "I'll just have coffee. Thanks." Dustin looked down at me. "Do you want something?"

"No," I said, shaking my head and smiling at him. I lowered my voice to a whisper. "Just being here with you is enough."

The waitress left, and Dustin and I sat there without saying a word, just looking into each other's eyes. I nearly forgot about Nick and Mimi and Mrs. Gray, until Mrs. Gray cleared her throat. "My word," she said, pretending to look out the window. "That fellow sure has a lot of stars and bars on his uniform. Tell me what they all mean, Dusty."

Dustin had to look away then, and he answered his mother's question while I seethed in silence. I knew it was wrong to want Dustin all to myself, but couldn't I have him for just five minutes?

We weren't allowed to drive Dustin to the plane, so we waved good-bye in a parking lot, where he piled his gear onto a bus. "Bye, Mom," he said, hugging Mrs. Gray. "Bye, Mimi." He gave his grandmother a quick hug, then turned and clapped Nick's hand. "Thanks for coming, man," he said, patting Nick on the shoulder with his free hand. "Take care, and write more than once a month, OK?"

Then he turned to me. The wind blew my hair over my eyes, but I didn't want to move it because Dustin would see I was crying. He clasped me to him, and I sobbed once, then I felt his strong hands in my hair. "Take good care of yourself, Cassiopeia

115

Perkins," he whispered. "And remember—I'm half-returned before I go. My heart will always be with you."

I couldn't answer—I knew I'd start bawling if I tried to talk—so I lifted my face to his for a quick kiss. He released me, picked up his gear, and turned again to wave at his mom and grandmom. They waved back, but I just stood there in the wind, tears running down my face.

14

A week or so later, Dustin wrote that Don Jackson, his friend from basic training, was also in his platoon at the Aberdeen Proving Grounds. They were becoming close friends, he said, and that was good because "a guy needed someone he could trust in the army." They spent most of their time either in classes or field training, and the time was passing faster than he'd hoped. By mid-February he'd be on his permanent base in Fort Hood, Texas. And after only eighteen more months, he'd be home.

"I'm counting the days 'till I see you again," he said as he closed off the letter. "It was so hard for me to say good-bye to you at the base—I don't think I could have gone through with it if not for this tough army training! I wanted more than anything to follow you back to the bus station and go home to Canova Cove where I belong. But a man has to keep his word, and I gave mine to the army—I'm theirs for two years. And I'm giving my word to you, Cassie. I'll love you forever."

I clutched the letter tightly and pressed it to my face. I thought I could smell a faint whiff of Dustin's after-shave, and I lay down on my bed, holding the pages close to my nose. His hand had written this; this paper had been warmed by his touch . . . maybe he had even held it to his lips for a kiss. Not many guys would do that, but Dustin would.

After a while I got up and reached for the box of stationery in my desk drawer. I was going to write a doozy of a letter in return, and Dustin would know how much I loved him, too. There was no one in the world like him, and I couldn't believe he was mine!

I had just licked the envelope when Max rapped on my door. "Cassie, I thought you should know about something," he said, hesitantly coming into my room. "The president of Madagascar, Emmanuel DuClaret, has openly invited U.S. forces to remain in his country. Our navy is sending three battleships to the waters outside Madagascar."

"Why?" I asked, crinkling my nose.

"There are several bloodthirsty Communist dictators in that part of the world who have terrorized African countries for years," Max said. "Apparently one of them, Jonas Bibene, is threatening Madagascar. He has established a political party there and oversees guerilla warfare from Nampula."

"From where? Speak English, Max."

Max took a deep breath to explain, and I waved my hand. "Forget it. Just tell me why the United States cares so much about Madagascar. What are we trying to do, protect the world's coffee and vanilla supply?"

"I think it may have more to do with the space tracking station that was closed several years ago," Max said, lifting an eyebrow. "Unless I miss my guess, the president of Madagascar has probably promised to return it. That would be a big score for our government."

I chewed on the edge of my fingernail. "Dustin won't have to go there, will he?"

Max shrugged. "That all depends on our president. And Jonas Bibene."

I had never heard of Jonas Bibene, but if Max said the story was true, I believed it. Max was smarter than any history professor I had ever had, and he spent hours on his computer tapping into data bases and news reports. I wouldn't be surprised if he had even tapped into the CIA!

But the situation in Madagascar worried me. Dustin had mentioned Madagascar in one of his letters. Max said that dictator guy, Bibene, was bloodthirsty. I only hoped our president wouldn't think a space tracking station was worth the life of Dustin Gray and other guys just like him.

I was surprised when Chip met me at my locker after school the next week. "I never see you anymore," he said, leaning against the lockers as I picked out the books I'd need for my homework. "What's going on, Cass?"

I shook my head. So much had happened, and I didn't feel exactly comfortable telling Chip, who used to be my boyfriend, about Dustin. Still . . . I paused as I remembered that Chip did know a lot about the Bible. And he had always been a good friend.

"I'm sorry I haven't called you or anything," I said. "And I'm glad you're here now." I slammed my locker shut, turning to look at him. "Can you walk me home? I've got something to ask you."

Chip nodded, and as we walked I told him about Dustin, about how we'd come to really care about each other. Chip listened without saying much, and I hoped his feelings weren't being hurt. But when I took a quick glance at his face, he didn't look upset or anything. Just interested. I took a breath, then asked him about some things that had been bothering me.

"Dustin is in the army with this guy who's telling him about Universalism. Do you know what that's all about?"

Chip nodded. "Universalism is the belief that all is one," he said, gesturing in the air with his free hand. "Universalists basically believe that God is the same thing as creation, that he's a principle, a universal law, energy." He smiled at me. "It may sound a little weird to you, but it's actually a common philosophy."

"Well, it doesn't sound all that strange. I mean, isn't that sort of true?" I asked. "You *can* see God in creation."

"In creation we see *evidence* of a Creator, that's true," Chip said, nodding. "But God is not a tree. He *created* the tree. God is a person, a personality, and he existed before creation. When this earth has come and gone, he will continue to exist."

"OK," I said, agreeing with him. "But Dustin told me his friend said that Jesus, Muhammad, and Buddha were all prophets of God, that they all point to the same God."

"That's not true," Chip said, shaking his head. "Jesus himself said that he is the only way to God. He even warns us in the Bible that others would come and claim to be the way to God, and he tells us to watch out for those people." Chip stopped and looked at me, and I could see how serious he was by the look on his face and in his eyes. "Cassie, Jesus of Nazareth is the unique, onetime, *only* Son of God. A lot of people just don't want to believe in him, so they call him just one more of the endless stream of gurus and teachers who are limited in their power. But he isn't."

"Dustin said his friend told him that people are basically good," I added, frowning. "And that we've all got part of God in us."

Chip smiled. "That'd be cool, but it's not true. The Bible tells us that even though we were created in the image of God, and though we have great value to God, humanity is fallen and sinful. We can't have God in us until we give our lives to him."

"Yeah," I agreed, nodding. "I see what you mean. But . . . how do I explain all of this to Dustin? It's hard enough in person, but I have to write all this in a letter!"

Chip's blue eyes smiled at me. "God wrote all these things to us in a letter," he said, pointing to the small Bible in his book bag. "I'm sure he won't mind if you quote from it. You know, Cassie, God loves Dustin, too. Even more than you do. Why not ask him to help you know what to write?"

"Sounds easy enough," I said, slowing down. We were at the park near my house, so I stopped and gave Chip a sharp salute. "I thank you, Dustin thanks you, and the U.S. Army thanks you."

Chip saluted back. "You'll do fine, Cassie. But, uh . . ." His eyes fell to the ground as if he were reluctant to continue. "How serious are you about this guy?"

I bit my lip, then spoke softly. "I . . . I think I really love him, Chip." Then I shrugged—this whole conversation suddenly felt too deep. I punched Chip in the shoulder. "But that doesn't mean I'm going to marry him or anything."

Chip surprised me by catching my hand and holding it. "Just do me a favor, Cassie. Be careful," Chip said, his eyes shining with concern. "Do you remember when Doug talked to our group about not dating someone who isn't a Christian? It's easy to fall in love with someone you enjoy, but real love isn't just a feeling, it's a commitment. And you shouldn't commit yourself to someone who doesn't know the Lord."

I felt myself blushing. "Good grief, I'm not getting married, Chip."

He smiled and let go of my hand. "Not yet. But the whole reason for dating is to find someone with whom you fit, right? Well, if you're dating someone who's not a Christian, you're shopping in the wrong size!"

"Oh yeah?" I said, crossing my arms. I was beginning to wonder if Chip had an ulterior motive for this little talk. "I suppose you know someone who'd fit just like a comfortable old shoe, right?"

Chip smiled, and the dimple in his cheek winked at me. "Maybe I do, maybe I don't," he said, teasingly. He reached forward and caught me in a brief, friendly hug. "Take care of yourself, Cass," he said. "And just think about this: Who means more to you—God, or your new boyfriend?"

He grinned at me once again and walked away.

15

Time seemed to fly by. On February 10, Private Dustin Gray was transferred to Fort Hood, Texas, a fully qualified United States soldier.

On February 14, I received a dozen roses and three pounds of chocolate from my soldier boyfriend.

On February 15, I got my first and last letter from Dustin in Texas. He was being shipped out to join his unit, the Thirteenth Coscom, currently supporting the First Cavalry Division in Madagascar.

"By the time you get this, I'll be on the big island, at least that's what we're all calling it," Dustin wrote. "Since I'll be the new kid on the base, I expect I'll be washing a lot of dishes. I have three comforting thoughts. One is that Don will be with me, so at least I'll know someone. The second is that at this base they're serving three hots a day, so I won't have to eat that prepackaged junk they call food. The third is that I'll still get your letters, so just send them to the Fort Hood address, and they'll forward the mail. Hang on, sweetie. I'll be home before you know it. I think I may get leave at Christmas. Love, Dustin."

I folded the letter and ran to Nick's room. "Quick, what are three hots a day?" I yelled.

Nick looked up from his history book and grinned. "Three hot meals, dummy."

"Dustin's in Madagascar," I said, showing him the letter.

Nick whistled. "Man, he's going to see action already! Boy, do I envy him!"

"How can you say that?" I couldn't believe Nick actually wanted to go to war and be surrounded by flying bullets. "Dustin's over there, putting his life in danger for his country, and you act like it's some big party!"

"He's not in danger," Nick said, laughing. "He's not an infantryman. He's not even a pilot, for heaven's sake. He repairs jeeps, Cassie. How dangerous do you think that is?"

I found a glimmer of hope in Nick's words. "It's not dangerous?"

"Not hardly," Nick answered, the corner of his mouth drooping. "He'll be safe and sound at the base. They've got a guard posted at night to keep the base safe, and three hot meals a day. What a life!"

I sighed in relief. Knowing that Dustin wasn't in the line of fire made me feel a lot better. Tomorrow I'd go over to his house and tell his mom and grandmom what Nick had told me. They were probably worried, too.

Dustin's letters were the highlights of my week. I would finish reading one and be ready for the next one to come. Nick gave me a hard time about being a "mailbox vulture," but I didn't care. I just wanted to know Dustin was safe.

One afternoon, there was another letter waiting for me when I got home from school. I dashed up to my room and tore it open.

> March 28
> Dear Cassie:
>
> I've been here on the big island of Madagascar six weeks now, and life has settled into a routine. Don and I get up early, eat breakfast, and then wash dishes for the rest of the company before going to work on the vehicles. It's not exactly glamorous. I can't wait until the next new guys get here, 'cause I'll be happy to give them this dishwashing job!
>
> Once we're out of the kitchen, we'll probably

pull guard duty outside the camp. That's not so bad. You just walk around the fence, or if you're lucky enough to be assigned to the guard shack, you just check I.D. papers and make sure no idiots drive loaded bombs into camp. (Just kidding!)

During the day we keep busy doing our jobs as wheeled vehicle repairmen. That has quite a ring to it, doesn't it? I keep wondering how it will look on my college application. Probably great. Anyway, I've been thinking about college. I think I'll major in English or journalism and be a novelist one day. I've seen enough weird things around here to fill ten books, and all I have to do is write one best-seller. How would you like to be the wife of a famous novelist?

Don and I went to a meeting off base last night. It was a group called "Children Who Love," and it was a wild mix of people, but they all seemed to really love each other. They held hands and sang gentle songs, and talked about love and peace and God. I thought they'd hate us 'cause we were in our uniforms, but one girl came up to me and said, "I know you're sworn to fight, but in your heart there is peace." I don't know if what she said made sense, but all the people were really meek and innocent-looking. Half of them looked like they were high on something, but Don just joined right in with them, closing his eyes and singing at the top of his lungs. When it was over, they invited us to come back.

Well, sweetie, I'll sign off now. At night when I fall into bed, I see your dark eyes shining there in the night, and I don't feel so lonely. Write to me soon, and tell Nick and your family hi for me.

All my love,
Dustin

I scanned his letter twice, but there wasn't one word about fighting or death. Did he think he was fooling me? The things Dustin left out of his letters were splashed across the newspaper and CNN continually. Four soldiers had died yesterday when their truck was bombed by terrorists, right in the center of Antananarivo, the capital. Three medical personnel were killed last week in Toliara, a small town on the coast.

Max said this war was a lot like Vietnam because the enemy was hidden. The soldiers couldn't tell if a little gray-haired lady ahead of them was somebody's grandma or a madwoman with a bomb. The enemy had no camps, no planes, and no uniformed army. They were sneaky and came out at night to kill unsuspecting soldiers as they slept.

Safe in Nampula, the dictator Jonas Bibene encouraged the killing. I didn't know anything about Bibene, but I prayed every night that God would stop him. I didn't care how it happened—whether it took an assassin, an earthquake, or even a tornado to suck him off the face of the earth! Surely God could do something to stop the man's evil before Dustin got hurt.

But Dustin apparently didn't see the danger. Maybe he had spent too much time washing dishes, but his letters made it sound as if he were on vacation in Madagascar, the home of loving people and pretty native girls who spoke French.

His next letter was different.

April 8
Dear Cassie:

Today three men from my unit were badly hurt when someone threw a hand grenade into the bar where they went to drink after work. They were airlifted out immediately, and I heard they'll be OK, but the attack surprised me. I have never really thought much about living . . . and dying. I could never write home about these things—my mom would flip—so I'm writing to you. Please don't show this letter to anyone. Nick would think I've grown soft, and my mom and grandmom would be scared. But I think you'll understand.

Is this all there is to life? Have you ever really thought about it? I don't know if you knew about this, but I had a little sister, April, who died when she was six. She drowned. Anyway, I remember thinking as a kid that her death didn't make sense. Why would God have given her life just for six years? What good was that? She was just a kid, and she hadn't even *done* anything yet—but her chance to live was gone, just like that. I turned my back to count to thirty for a game of hide-and-seek, and she was gone forever.

I've lived nineteen years—thirteen years longer than April—but I really don't feel like I've done anything with my life, either. I've been so busy going to school, learning, and try-ing to please my mom that I haven't had a chance to do anything for me! Do you know what I mean? Even *you've* done more than I have—you've traveled, cut a record, and met hundreds more people than I have. I just can't help feeling that if someone throws a grenade in my path tomorrow, my life will have been a big waste. Everything I've done has been to prepare me for the future, but what if there is no future? Even loving you is something I do for the future. But what if I never see you again? I hate to think you've wasted your time waiting for me.

Well, I don't want to be depressing, but I needed to get these things off my chest. I promise I'll never be this morbid again. Don't tell anyone about this, OK? Take care, sweetie, and send me one of your wonderful letters soon. I could really use one about now.

Loving you now and always,
Dustin

I slowly folded Dustin's letter and placed it under my pillow. For the first time I was beginning to realize how different we were. Dustin sounded so lost, so alone! His thoughts were filled with hopelessness, and while I might get depressed sometimes, I hadn't felt really hopeless since I'd trusted God with my future. I wanted to help Dustin understand that kind of trust, but how could I do that when he was thousands of miles away?

There was only one way. I pulled my box of stationery from my desk drawer—there were two pale pink sheets left. I'd have to go to the store and get more, but this letter wouldn't wait. If two pages weren't enough, I'd write on whatever I could find, even grocery bags. I pulled out my special pen, clicked it, and began to write.

April 20
Dear Dustin:

First, I don't mind that you poured out your feelings to me. That's what friends are for, right? To listen to everything, even the stuff that doesn't sound so good when we spill it out.

I'm glad you wrote what you did, because I've been wanting to tell you something. I just wasn't sure how to do it. I'm still not too sure how to say this right, but here goes.

Dustin, I don't think you'll be able to see any meaning to life until you understand who gave you life. I know you've been thinking a lot about God lately. Well, I want you to know the same God I do, the real God. No, I don't worship the God of Buddha or of whatever guru is hanging around your camp. I worship the God who created the universe. He's real, and he sent his Son, Jesus, who was a real person, to die for our sins because Jesus is the only way we can ever hope to reach God. And without reaching God, without giving him control of your life and trusting him, Dustin, I'm afraid there really is no meaning to life.

It's like this—God created us to have fellowship with him. You know, to love him. I mean, he loves us! More than we can ever imagine. You know how Don told you that we all have some God in us? I'm sorry, but that's not true. What we *do* all have, what we are born with, are sinful tendencies. And our sin is what keeps us from God.

I know you told me that you believe in God and Jesus. That's good. But you need more than belief. My brother Max explained it to me this way:

I believe the president of the United States is real. I know he *exists*, because I've seen his picture and seen him on TV. Just like you know God exists because you've seen the world, his creation. I also believe in what the president stands for. I *agree* with him and, if I were old enough to vote, I'd have voted for him. I'd listen to him and do what he suggests. I'd trust him. That's how much you need to believe in

God. You need to agree with him that you need him, and that sin has come between you.

But I *don't* believe in the president enough to bet my life on him. If terrorists captured my house and my family and held us hostage, do I believe that the president of the United States would show up on my doorstep to save me, even if he had to risk his own life? (I believe *you'd* do that, Dusty, but I don't think the Pres would.) No way!

That's the kind of belief and trust that I do have in God. I know he would risk his life to save me. He already did. He loves me so much that he sent Jesus, who was God *and* man, to die for me. Jesus gave his life as payment for the wrongs I have done. I really *believe* in God. I trust him enough to place my life in his hands and, if I were to die tomorrow, I know I would be with him, and it would be enough for me to know that I had done all he wanted me to do.

Plus, I know that life doesn't end when our bodies stop breathing. There's a heaven out there, Dustin, and I'll be there with God! Forever! If I live seventy years or only sixteen, it doesn't matter. I mean, what is that compared to an eternity with God?

Dustin, if you want peace about the things

that are bothering you, you need to believe in God. Really believe. Put-your-life-on-the-line believe. Like I said at the beginning of this letter, I've been wanting to write you about these things for a long time. I just couldn't find the words and I wasn't sure you'd understand. But if you can't understand these things, you can't really understand me. You may even think I'm a little crazy.

If I didn't care about you, I wouldn't say anything. But I care. A lot. So here's my letter. If you think I'm nuts and want to break up, OK. I really shouldn't have let our relationship go this far, I think, without talking about these things. I don't want to hurt you. But my life is in God's hands, and he has to come first for me. I guess what I'm needing to know is this: Where is God in your life? Let me know what you think.

Much love,
Cassie

16

Three weeks went by before I heard from Dustin again. I had just about decided that he never wanted to talk to me again (why does talking about Jesus rub a lot of people the wrong way?), but then a tattered letter arrived in the mail. I snatched it off the hall table and raced upstairs to my room to read it.

May 4
Dear Cassie:

Don is dead. It took me a long time to get over it. I couldn't face his death myself, let alone tell anyone else about it, so I'm sorry I haven't written. But here I am again, unburdening myself to you and you alone.

Don and I had guard duty last month, and we were lucky and pulled the guard shack.

That's easy duty—you just sit in the shack and wait for cars or Jeeps to pull through the gates, then you check ID papers or whatever. It was a Monday night, about nine-thirty, and I had just finished reading Don your letter about God. I was upset—I couldn't believe you really had thought about breaking off our relationship.

Don laughed and asked if you were what he called a "fun-damn-mentalist." He said you must be one of those people who believes God sends people to hell and takes all the fun out of life. He told me to forget about you, and for a minute, I actually listened to him. My feelings were hurt, Cass.

But then I told him you weren't like that. He just waved me away and lit up a joint (he'd gotten it from some locals). I stood by the window because I was upset at him for talking about you like that, but I was confused, too, Cassie. You were thousands of miles away, and Don, my buddy, was right there next to me. I don't know if you'll understand, but right then I wanted to believe him and not you.

We sat for an hour without saying much. Don was smoking and getting pretty stoned, so I opened the window to get some fresh air. I saw a vehicle approaching from the south and told Don that someone was coming. I should have known that he was in no condition to go outside, but he staggered to his feet, slung his rifle over his shoulder, and went out to meet the approaching car. That's when he made the mistake. We're supposed to keep the gate closed until we've seen some identification, but Don pressed the button to open the gate and then waved his hand for the Jeep to stop.

It was an army Jeep, but it wasn't a soldier behind the wheel. It was a man wearing a turban. He slowed just enough for Don to walk out to him, then stepped on the gas and waved a machine gun. I yelled and pounded on the button to close the gate, but the Jeep was already halfway through. It just roared on by, hitting Don as it passed through the gate. Don spun away from the Jeep like a rag doll, and the enemy drove the Jeep through the camp, spraying machine-gun fire everywhere.

I don't think Don knew what hit him. I managed to get to the phone and call security, and they caught the guy in the turban before anyone else was hurt. That was a miracle. But Don lay outside on the ground, and when I ran to him, there was only a trickle of blood coming from his mouth to show that anything was wrong. His face was all screwed up in pain, though, and he gasped when he saw me coming. I tried to pick him up, and I told him the medics were coming. He grabbed my shirt and pulled me down to him. "I'm hurt real bad," he said. "I think I'm gonna die."

I told him he was crazy. "No way, Gray," he said, just like he used to in basic training. "This is it. And I'm scared, Gray, I'm scared."

His hand shook, and his eyes were wide with fright. I know you never met him, Cassie, but Don was one tough dude. I'd never seen even a trace of fear in him, yet there he was in my arms, shaking and crying like a baby. The worst part of it was that I didn't know what to do or say.

I told him he shouldn't be afraid. He was always telling me about reincarnation, and how he was going to come back as a flower or something, so I told him not to worry. "You had it all figured out, man," I told him. "Remember the flower?"

He cursed at me and told me I was crazy. "That stuff is garbage, man," he said. I was just staring at him, when his pupils suddenly went really wide and I thought he was a goner. It was like he didn't see me anymore, like he saw something else there, and he screamed that they were coming for him. I yelled, "Right! Right! The ambulance is coming for you, Jackson!" But he arched his back and kept screaming while I yelled that everything would be all right.

The ambulance pulled up then and took him away. But I'm pretty sure he was dead by the time they loaded him into the back. After a while two other guys came to relieve me of my post, and I spent the next four hours in the commanding officer's office, thinking I was going to be court-martialed for allowing that Jeep onto the base. But they figured Don was responsible, I guess, 'cause they let me off with a warning.

I didn't get off easy, though, Cass. Don was dead, and I had watched him die—and I saw that everything he had ever told me was one big lie. He sure didn't believe any of it. I guess his philosophy was fine for living, for giving you freedom to do your own thing, but his religion didn't make sense when it came time for him to die.

I think I'm changing, Cassie, and that scares me a lot. I'm not the same guy you knew last summer. I've been thinking about what you wrote in your last letter, about what Don said, and about what everyone else around me says. You believe that God loves everyone, but for all Don's talk, I don't think he really loved God. He loved the *idea* of God, but he didn't really love God.

So last week, I was walking along the fence on guard duty, and I couldn't take it anymore. I lifted my eyes to the night sky and asked God if he could hear me. I listened, real hard, but I couldn't hear him—just the waves beating on the shore that's not too far from here. Still, in my heart, for some reason, I knew God was listening. So I told God I wanted to believe in him, that I wanted to put my life in his hands. I said it. I meant it.

I talked to God for a long time. I told him all the things you had written in your letter. I wanted to really believe in him, no matter what. So now I'm writing to tell you that my life is God's, and I don't know anymore if I'm supposed to marry you when I come home. I feel peaceful inside—about us, about everything—but I'm not going to be selfish and ask you to wait for me or anything like that. That's not fair. Besides, you have to do what God wants you to do, too. And, like I said, I'm not the same guy you knew last summer.

But whatever happens, I'll always love you, Cassie, because you loved me enough to tell me what believing in God is really all about. I can never repay you for that.

Love,
Dustin

17

I kept writing Dustin. I had to and I wanted to. First, he needed me more than ever because not only had he lost his best friend; he had just become a Christian. I knew he'd need encouragement. Second, I wrote him because I still loved him. He had changed and become more serious—I could see it in his letters—but he was still the wonderful guy I had known all along.

On Thanksgiving Uncle Jacob pulled out the turkey platter again and roasted a huge bird, enough for fifteen people. I asked Mom and Tom if we could invite Mrs. Gray and Dustin's grandmother, and they thought it was a good idea.

I called Mrs. Gray, half expecting her to refuse. So when she said, "Thank you, Cassie. Mother and I would like to come," and her tone of voice was even nice, I almost dropped the phone in surprise. I hung up slowly, smiling to myself. Maybe Mrs. Gray had figured that since I'd stuck with Dustin for over a year, I wasn't going to dump him for the rich guy she was always worrying about.

When Mrs. Gray and Mimi came over for Thanksgiving dinner, they were decked out in their Sunday best. I met them at the door and gave Mimi a hug. She smiled and patted my cheek. "Such a sweet girl," she said.

Mrs. Gray and I stood awkwardly for a minute, looking at each other. Then I stepped forward and hugged her, too. She kind of stiffened for a second, then I could feel her relax, and she carefully hugged me back. When we stepped away from each other, she smiled at me. It was the first time she'd ever looked like Dustin.

We all gathered together around the table, and Tom said the blessing. Then Uncle Jacob cut the turkey.

"Who wants the drumstick?" Uncle Jacob asked, looking around at all of us. "Nick? Can you eat all of this?"

"Not me," Nick said, shaking his head. "Only Dustin can eat that much. Let's save it for him."

"He may get leave to come home for Christmas," Mrs. Gray said, turning pink with pleasure. All of the frostiness was gone from her smile, and she seemed to be really happy to share Thanksgiving with us. I guess she was learning that people who lived in big houses were real people, too.

"That's great," Uncle Jacob said, winking at Mrs. Gray. "We can just toss those drumsticks in the freezer until then."

We all laughed, and Uncle Jacob cut a generous portion of breast meat for Mimi. Suddenly Max's head shot up and his eyes widened. He pulled an earplug from his ear. "Quick, to the living room," he said, pushing back his chair. "The smart house system just told me there's a special news report on channel 8. Hurry!"

We left the Thanksgiving dinner on the table and stampeded into the living room. The television had come on by itself, and the "Special Report" emblem filled the screen. Then the news anchor smiled at us from behind his desk.

"Good afternoon," Dan Rather said, his sober face looking unusually pleasant. "Good news today from Madagascar. The president of the republic, Emmanuel DuClaret, has just won that country's national election. The United States' peacekeeping forces are no longer needed, says President DuClaret, and congress has authorized the return of all United States military personnel."

Rather looked directly into the camera. "Our

American men and women are coming home," he said. "General Burba predicts that all American troops will be back on United States soil by Christmas."

As everyone cheered and clapped, I reached for Dribbles and hugged him so tightly that he snorted in protest. Dustin was coming home! He was out of danger! This would be the best Christmas of my life!

"Cassie, will you hand me that box?" Mom said, pointing to a battered shoe box at my feet.

"Sure, Mom." I lifted the lid. Inside were the tin ornaments that had been on every Perkins Christmas tree since I was two. I laughed and slid them across the carpet to her.

Max sat on the floor next to me, methodically untangling the strings of electric lights. "Can't you get the smart house to do that for you?" I teased him.

"No," Max answered, ignoring my attempt at humor. "But I can program the house computer to turn the lights on and off. I can also make them twinkle."

"Great." I looked up as Mom placed the first ornament on the tall tree Tom had picked up for our living room. "Shouldn't we wait for Nick to get home? He might want to help."

Mom shook her head. "He'll go straight from school to the gym and won't get home until supper," she said. "I don't want to wait that long. I like to have my tree up and finished early."

I sighed. The first of December seemed almost too soon to put up the tree, but Mom was planning several Christmas parties, and she always wanted the house to look absolutely stunning before the people started pouring in. Our house at Christmas was like something out of *House Beautiful*. Mom burned scented candles that filled the house with the smells of gingerbread and cinnamon, and she hung huge wreaths and glittery swags above every window and doorway. Tom said marrying an interior decorator was the smartest thing he ever did, especially at Christmas.

This year I wanted the house to look extra special. Dustin was coming home.

We had written each other stacks of letters through the months, and every reason I had ever had for *not* wanting to fall in love with him was gone. He was growing stronger in his faith every week. He wrote that he had met a chaplain on the base who was leading a small Bible study for the soldiers, and Dustin went every week without fail. Now he probably knew more than I did about the Bible.

The hurtful memories of his past had healed, and

149

Dustin said that he was finally able to trust God with his guilt about what happened when April drowned years ago, and about what had happened to Don that night at the guard shack. I sighed. As much as Dustin seemed to want to take the blame for Don's death, it wasn't his fault—and I was glad when he finally realized that.

My mom and Tom even realized that my relationship with Dustin was something special. They didn't tease me about him like they teased me about my other boyfriends. Mom didn't even nag me about staying home too much. I did go out a lot with Chip and Nick and Andrea, but everyone at school and in my family knew my heart was miles away in Madagascar.

I opened another shoe box and found my favorite ornaments, the ones Dad had made one year from bread dough. The first Christmas after the divorce I couldn't bear to even look at those ornaments; now I laughed when I saw them. One was a rocket ship with "Maxwell One" written down the side, and another was a caricature of me as a chubby opera singer, my mouth open in a wide *O*. There was even a dough version of a Chinese pug, but the name on the dog's collar was Suki, not Dribbles. Suki, the dog I had when Dad lived with us, had been hit by a car and killed. Dribbles was a present from Tom.

"Life goes on," I murmured, not really caring who heard me. I put the dough ornaments on the tree, and Mom smiled when I caught her watching me.

"Indeed it does," she answered, then she turned back to decorating the tree.

When the tree glistened and glimmered in all its glory, I ran upstairs to my room and pulled out a new box of Christmas stationery. "Joy to the World!" was written across the top, and under that, I wrote, ". . . and Joy to You, Too!"

Dearest Dustin:

This will be the last letter I write before you come home, so I wanted it to be extra-special. The house is being decorated, Uncle Jacob's busy baking cookies (you should *smell* them), and I've got an extra-wonderful present for you downstairs under the Christmas tree. It's something every soldier needs and something you'll put to good use.

I'm so proud of you, Dusty! Your mom called the other day and said you got some kind of award for helping pull a guy out of a burning Jeep. I told her I wasn't surprised. You've always been my knight in shining armor, and I knew that's the kind of thing you'd do. So, to commemorate your

award, I've written a poem for you. A Cassie
Perkins Original. Enjoy.

The Glory of Love
Like a knight in shining armor,
Or so the story goes,
You stepped into my life one day,
And now my glad heart knows
That you and I were meant to be
Like kindred souls, apart
For just a little while, you see,
While God adjusts our hearts.
While God molds us to fit his plan
Our love grows stronger still,
Together or apart, you know,
We still can do his will.

I do not understand at all
The wonders God can do.
I stand amazed at this great thought:
God's love sent me to you.
That truly is his greatest gift—
Not that I love you so—
But that God gave his love so great
To us to share and know.

Love always and hurry home!
Cassie

18

"Cassie!" Mom's voice rang up the stairs, and I stuck my head out my bedroom door.

"What?"

"Mail gram for you," Mom said, waving an envelope in the air. "Air mail."

I ran out of my room so fast that Dribbles woke up and started barking like the house was on fire. A mail gram! Maybe Dustin was coming home even earlier than I had thought! He was due home on December 20, in just one week, but maybe he had earned a special pass or something.

I took the envelope from Mom and was surprised to see that it wasn't addressed in Dustin's handwriting. The return address told me the mail gram was from Chaplain Mike Mastings of the United States Army.

Mom's eyes were dark and a little worried when I looked up at her, so I smiled as I moved past her into the quiet of the den. "Dustin told me about this chaplain," I said, reassuring her. "They're good friends."

But when I sank into the overstuffed wing chair and tore the edges of the letter open, my fingers were trembling. Why was the chaplain writing to me? The letter was dated December 12, noon, Madagascar. Its thin blue paper was covered in neat lines of block printing. I took a deep breath and began to read.

Dear Cassie:

I feel as if I know you because Dustin Gray has told me much about you. It is therefore with both great sorrow and great joy that I write this letter to you: Sorrow because Dustin was seriously injured this morning in what seems to be a senseless act; joy because Dustin was hurt performing an act of unusual courage, love, and devotion.

As you know, hostilities have ceased, and we soldiers are packing up to go home. Unfortunately, the terrorist activity has not ceased just because the president of this country has remained in power. We are no longer obligated to be here, but this country is certainly not free from problems.

Dustin was packing, excited about seeing you, his mother, and his grandmother soon. He showed me the stack of letters you had sent him so faithfully, and I know he read them over and over. You were a great encouragement to him, especially after he gave his life to Jesus Christ. Some of the other guys didn't understand his commitment, but he knew you did. He showed me the most recent letter you wrote him, the one with the poem, just this morning before we left the base. He kept it in his little army-issue Testament.

This morning Dustin and his unit had liberty—free time—in the town of Antsirabe, a small town not far from the capital. I went along because Dustin and I usually went to have coffee and talk.

We were in a small café in town near the crowded village market. Dustin always likes watching the people because they are so colorful and so different from Americans. One little boy in particular caught his eye—he was an African boy with large, dark eyes and a most appealing smile. The boy seemed to fall in love with big Dustin from the first minute. He wouldn't let go of his mother's hand, but he kept looking over at Dustin and smiling. They played a game of peek-a-boo for about ten minutes, then the boy and his mother went into a small shop across the street.

They had been inside the shop for about ten minutes while Dustin and I talked, then suddenly there was an explosion. The windows of the building across the street blew almost into our faces, and glass and wood and rubble flew everywhere. I saw the lifeless body of the boy's mother in the street in front of us, and before I could say anything, Dustin was out of his chair and halfway across the road.

Some village men tried to hold him back, but they were no match for Dustin's strength. He ran into the charred and burning remains of the building, and a minute later his big, sooty hands lowered the boy out of a hole in the wall. The child was choking and crying, but he was all right. One of the villagers ran up, grabbed him, and rushed him away from the fire.

But the heat was intense, and the doorway where Dustin had entered was, by that time, totally blocked by flames. Dustin was too big to climb out through the hole from which the boy had escaped. The firemen did get Dustin out, Miss Perkins, but he was badly burned. The army has notified his mother and grandmother, of course, but I thought you should know about the accident, too. Dustin risked his life today, not in the service of his country, but in the service of God—for a poor little boy with dancing black eyes and an eager smile. Not many men would have done that, and you can be very proud of him.

I'm afraid Dustin will spend Christmas, as well as the next few months, in a VA hospital near Charlottesville, Virginia. When he is in a more stable condition, he will probably be transferred to the Veterans Hospital in St. Petersburg, Florida, where I am sure you will be able to visit him. His recovery will undoubtedly take many months.

I am sorry that I must write this so near to Christmas, but I hope your holiday will be blessed as you remember the gift Dustin gave today: the gift of life.

Sincerely,
Chaplain Mike Mastings
United States Army

My first thought was that this letter was a horrible joke. One of Mom's Christmas records was playing on the stereo, and the words of the song floated idly into my mind: "I'll be home for Christmas, you can count on me. . . ." Of course Dustin would be home soon! Just like all the other soldiers who would be home for Christmas with their friends and family.

Then I remembered the news reports of casualties in Madagascar, and I knew we were lucky that Dustin was alive. Other families weren't so fortunate. There were Christmas trees with presents that would never be opened . . . stockings that wouldn't get turned upside down in a mad rush . . . kisses that wouldn't be claimed under the mistletoe.

At our house, nobody would eat the drumsticks on our Christmas turkey this year. We'd throw them in the freezer with the drumsticks from Thanksgiving. If it took two years, I'd save them for Dustin.

I leaned back in the chair, my heart aching at the thought of Dustin in pain. "Why, God?" I whispered. "Why did you let the terrorist throw a grenade right in front of Dustin? Couldn't someone else have helped that kid?"

As much as I wanted an easy answer, I knew I wouldn't find one. Dustin had never found an easy answer to the questions about why his sister drowned or why his father walked out. What he had found was peace. Would I?

Nick came into the den, whistling along with the record, but he stopped suddenly when he saw me sitting there. I didn't say anything, but I didn't have to. The letter from Chaplain Mastings had fallen from my hand to the floor, and Nick picked it up, read it, and then threw it to the ground as if it stung him.

"Oh, man!" Nick yelled, his voice filled with pain, his face turning red in anger. "Stupid, stupid Dustin! What'd he do that for? Nobody runs into a burning building, nobody at all—"

Mom had slipped into the room and she picked up the letter and skimmed it as Tom stood behind her. Max came in, too, and looked questioningly at Mom. "Dustin was badly hurt, honey," she told Max, her voice cracking. "He ran into a burning building to save a little boy's life."

"He's too strong to be badly hurt," Max said automatically. He pointed to a big box under the tree. "He'll be home soon, right? I spent two weeks making him a present. He's got to come here and open it."

"He won't be home for a long time," Tom said slowly, shaking his head. "I've heard of burn patients that require up to two years of surgery and rehabilitation to recover. I'm sorry, kids, but Dustin has a long, hard road ahead of him."

I didn't say anything. Neither did Nick. He just spun around and ran out of the room, and I ran after him.

19

We drove the Mustang all over town, and Nick's driving scared me. More than once I put my hand on his arm to slow him down. He obeyed, but he drove without saying a word as tears poured down his cheeks. I didn't know what to say. I was hurt; Nick was angry.

Nick finally parked the car under the tall pine trees at our neighborhood park. He got out and grabbed his basketball from the backseat. As he walked to the court, I covered my eyes with my hand and whispered a prayer: "God, please be with Dustin now, and help him not to feel much pain. And please, God, help Nick. He doesn't understand, God, and I don't know what to say."

Nick pounded the ball on the court, running, jumping, and shooting like a wild man. At first he was alone, but within a few minutes a couple of other guys had joined him, and they were fast setting up a game. I buried my face in my hands. How like a guy—when in a crisis, play ball!

I got out of the car and walked slowly around the park, ignoring the little kids on the swings and the older men playing softball in the late afternoon sun. There was a tall stand of trees that bordered the far edge of our park, and when I reached the trees I sat in the shady stillness and had the cry of my life, thinking about my dreams and Dustin's dreams and how quickly life could change.

Poor Dustin! I knew he had to be in a lot of pain. And he'd probably be scarred for life. Would I ever be able to look at him and see the strong, good-looking guy I had learned to love? Or would he look different—even horrible?

I was afraid, not only for Dustin in the hospital, but for me. I thought I really loved him, but did I? Would my love be strong enough to support Dustin during his difficult recovery? I didn't know. But one thing was for sure: I was going to find out.

Finally, when I couldn't cry anymore, I wiped my eyes on my shirt and stood up to go find Nick.

"You undercut me, man, and cost me the ball," a big red-haired boy shouted at Nick. He advanced until he was within five inches of Nick's face. "It's our ball. Hand it over."

Nick stood defiantly, the basketball resting loosely on his hip, but his eyes gleamed in anger. "I did not foul you, Carmen," he said, a sharp edge to his voice.

I looked at the other boy sharply. Carmen? This was the guy who had been harassing Nick all summer—the guy Dustin had stopped from clobbering Nick. My heart pounded. Why did this guy have to be here now, when Nick was already on the edge?

Nick just stood there, looking at the larger boy. "It's our ball, Carmen, and I'm not going to hand it over."

"Why not?" Carmen snarled, blood rushing to his face. "You'd better or you won't live to regret it."

The other boys backed away slowly, and I held my breath. The verbal attack had been bad enough, but it looked as though Nick and Carmen were going to trade more than words—again. In Nick's state of mind, I didn't doubt that he'd start a fight, and maybe he'd carry it farther than a black eye this time.

"I know you, Carmen," Nick said calmly. I was surprised at how steady his voice was. "And I'm getting a little tired of messing with you."

"I know you, too," Carmen answered, smiling contemptuously. "And I know I gave you a great shiner not too long ago. You want another one?

Or are you going to call that big guy to stop the fight before you get really hurt? What is he, your nanny?"

"He was my friend, Dustin Gray," Nick said, and I felt a sharp pain when Nick used the past tense. Good grief, Dustin wasn't dead! "And he's more of a man than you'll ever be." Nick resolutely bounced the ball to a boy behind him. "I'm not going to fight you, but it's our ball. And if you're smart, you'll stop making trouble here. We're not going to take it from you anymore."

The other guys behind Nick murmured in agreement, and Carmen looked around in confusion. "Nick's right, it's our ball," someone said, and one of the other guys added, "Yeah. Play fair, Carmen, or don't play at all."

Carmen scowled, paused for a moment, then backed down and stepped away from Nick. I let my breath out in relief, not even aware I'd been holding it.

"Nick," I called. "Don't you think it's time we went home? I want to go see Mrs. Gray."

"Sure, yeah," Nick said, coming with me. He left his friends—and Carmen—standing on the court.

Mom and Tom were waiting for us in the kitchen. "I thought you'd like to go with me," she said, gathering her purse. "Uncle Jacob and I whipped some casseroles together to take to Dustin's mother. They must be in a state of shock over there."

Tom cleared his throat awkwardly. "Uh, kids, I know these things are hard to understand," he said. "Right now it might seem impossible. But accidents happen in life, and we either go through them or grow through them. And if you start to feel sorry for yourself, just think of Dustin. He'll need you to be strong for him."

"It's OK, Tom," I said softly. He was trying hard to make me feel better, but there just wasn't any easy way to do it. "Dustin wasn't in an accident. He chose to help that kid. He saw someone who needed him, and he couldn't just stand there."

I wiped my cheek and was a little surprised to find that I was crying again. I knew I'd probably cry a lot in the next few days as I prayed for Dustin and tried to think of what to write him. I mean, what do you write someone who's been badly burned? *Sorry to hear about your misfortune?* Or *What the heck did you think you were doing?* I shook my head.

Nick looked up at Tom. "I'm going to go clean up," he said. "You all go over to the Grays' without me."

Nick and I went upstairs together, and I grabbed Nick's hand and squeezed it as we climbed. "Dustin would have been proud of you today," I said, looking up at him. "You handled that problem at the court without a fight. That's what Dustin would have done."

"Yeah." Nick gave me a weak smile. "I know. But when he's better, we're going to go back there and show that Carmen guy how to play some serious hoop."

"I know you will," I said, as Nick moved away.

The Grays' house was a scene of confusion when Mom, Max, and I arrived. Mrs. Gray had her suitcase on the sofa with piles of rumpled clothes scattered all around, and Mimi sat in her favorite chair with the television off. In her lap she was holding the old picture of Dustin with his mom, dad, and sister. A bravely decorated Christmas tree stood in the corner of the room.

Mrs. Gray let us in and stood quietly while my mom and I hugged her. "I was sorry to hear about Dustin's accident," Mom said, rumpling Max's hair as if grateful that *her* son was home and healthy. "We brought a couple of casseroles and a pie. . . . I didn't think you'd feel much like cooking."

"Thank you," Mrs. Gray said, closing the door behind us. "But I'm packing to go to Charlottesville. The army said I could visit Dusty, and I've taken two weeks off to go and be with him. I'm waiting on standby for an available flight. The airports are so crowded at Christmas. . . ." Her voice trailed off, but her eyes met my mother's and filled with tears. "I'm sure you understand."

"I do." My mother nodded, and she looked like she was about to cry, too.

"Mimi will need someone to visit her," I said, sitting on the footstool next to her chair. I looked into Mimi's eyes, which were dark and magnified by her glasses. "I'd be happy to come over every day and check on you—make sure you take your pills, eat dinner with you, and whatever."

Mrs. Gray smiled a genuine smile of appreciation. "Would you? Cassie, you don't know how much that would help me. I've been so busy worrying about Dusty that I nearly forgot about Mimi. I wasn't sure what I was going to do. You can't leave an eighty-nine-year-old woman alone for two weeks."

"I'll be just fine." Mimi spoke up, her chin raised. But her eyes twinkled and she patted my hand. "I'd like to have Dusty's girlfriend drop over. We can watch my programs together."

"Have the doctors told you anything new about Dustin's condition?" my mom asked Mrs. Gray. "We only know what Chaplain Mastings wrote Cassie."

Mrs. Gray nodded. "He has serious burns over his

hands, arms, and neck," she said, her chin quivering. "But, thank goodness, his clothing spared most of his skin, though he lost most of his hair. The doctors say they'll repair the damage with skin grafts, then Dusty will have to go through rehabilitation to be able to use his hands again. But the doctors say he's strong, and he'll be fine when they're finished."

"How long will rehabilitation take?" Max wanted to know.

Mrs. Gray shook her head. "A long while, I'm afraid. Skin only grows so quickly, and it's a process that can't be rushed. But if I know Dusty, he'll work hard. I just can't wait to have him here in Florida where we can visit him. We'll just take things one day at a time."

"One day at a time," I echoed. Her words had the profound ring of good sense. I didn't know what the future held for me and Dustin, but that was OK. I would let God hold Dustin *and* the future. I only had to take care of things one day at a time.

Mrs. Gray came over to me and laid her hands on my cheeks. "Thank you, Cassie Perkins," she said, "for being someone special to my son. He wrote me many times that your letters meant a great deal to him. I didn't realize how much that meant to me until—"

Her eyes filled with tears, and she patted my

cheek awkwardly. "Well, let's just say that life has a way of making you see things more clearly."

Then she leaned forward and kissed me on the forehead. I was surprised, but pleased, too.

"I guess we had better be going so you can finish packing," my mom told Mrs. Gray. She pulled Max toward her, and I stood up and pulled a brightly wrapped package out of my big purse.

"I was going to mail this, but since you'll be seeing Dustin soon, will you give it to him?" I asked, giving her the box. "It's his Christmas present." I felt myself blushing as Mrs. Gray took it. "It's a Bible. I know he has a little New Testament that the army gave him, but I thought he'd like something bigger."

Mrs. Gray smiled and rubbed her hand over the cheerful wrapping paper. "I'm sure he'll love it," she said. "I can read it to him in the hospital."

"That would be nice," Mom said.

I ducked my head. "Tell him I'll read it to him when he comes home to Florida, OK? I wish I'd had time to write him a letter, but tell him I miss him, OK? And that I wish I was there with him, and that we'll get through this, and that I'll be praying for him—" I stopped talking because my throat was all tight and I knew if I said one more word the tears hanging in my eyes would come pouring out.

Mrs. Gray looked at me for a moment in silence—

I saw that her eyes were full of tears, too—then she reached out and hugged me again. I drew a deep breath and hugged her back.

Finally Mom, Max, and I moved toward the door. As we walked to the car, I paused by the mailbox, trying to visualize Dustin's pleasure when he opened my present. He'd exclaim over the smooth leather cover where his name was embossed in gold, and he'd be pleased to find the Bible was in everyday language that he could understand. Then he'd open to the front page, where just this afternoon I had written something special:

To DUSTIN GRAY,
with love from Cassie Perkins at Christmas

Like a knight in shining armor,
Or so the story goes,
You stepped into my life one day,
And now my glad heart knows
That you and I were meant to be
Like kindred souls, apart
For just a while, you see,
While God adjusts our hearts.
While God molds us to fit His plan,
Our love grows stronger still.
Together or apart, you know,

We still can do his will.
And now you know the greatest gift,
God's love, sent from above.
You, by example, illustrate
The true glory of love.

Mom gently tapped the horn in farewell to Mrs. Gray, and I got in the car to go home.